# Teaching With Favorite
# Arnold Lobel
## Books

◆ ✳ ◆

BY ELLEN GEIST AND ELLEN TARLOW

NEW YORK • TORONTO • LONDON • AUCKLAND • SYDNEY
MEXICO CITY • NEW DELHI • HONG KONG • BUENOS AIRES

**Teaching** *Resources*

To my daughter, Sasha,
with gratitude for your insight
and invaluable assistance.

—E. G.

To my husband, Bruce,
for loving the stories as much as I do
and for being (just a little bit)
like Toad.

—E. T.

We wish to thank our editor, Deborah Schecter,
for her careful attention and significant contributions to this book.
And of course, we are indebted to Arnold Lobel
for the enduring inspiration of his wonderful stories.

Cover from FROG AND TOAD ARE FRIENDS by Arnold Lobel. Copyright © 1970 by Arnold Lobel. Used by permission of HarperCollins Publishers.

Cover from MOUSE SOUP by Arnold Lobel. Copyright © 1977 by Arnold Lobel. Used by permission of HarperCollins Publishers.

Cover from OWL AT HOME by Arnold Lobel. Copyright © 1975 by Arnold Lobel. Used by permission of HarperCollins Publishers.

"What Do I See in the Dark?" by Kathleen M. Hollenbeck. Copyright © 2005 by Kathleen M. Hollenbeck. Used by permission of the author.

Cover and interior design by Kathy Massaro
Interior art by Maxie Chambliss, except page 34 by James Graham Hale, and page 70 by Mark Hicks.
Photo, page 6, courtesy of HarperCollins Publishers

ISBN: 0-439-29461-4
Copyright © 2005 by Ellen Geist and Ellen Tarlow.
Published by Scholastic Inc.
All rights reserved.
Printed in the U.S.A.

1 2 3 4 5 6 7 8 9 10    40    13 12 11 10 09 08 07 06 05

# Contents

# Arnold Lobel in Your Classroom

To study Arnold Lobel is to open your classroom up to a gentle world of charming and quirky animal characters, whimsical humor, delight in nature, simple, satisfying storytelling, and much more. A favorite of both children and teachers, Lobel's books are easy and engaging enough for all children to appreciate but have an underlying richness and sophistication that make them particularly satisfying to reread and explore.

Lobel's books are a wonderful resource for teaching. His characters' childlike curiosity about the world makes cross-curricular connections a natural. Whether it is Owl getting mad at the moon for following him or Toad trying all the wrong things to make plants grow, the lovable misconceptions of his characters create many learning opportunities in science, language arts, social studies, and other content areas.

But first and foremost Arnold Lobel is a great storyteller. A contemporary link in the tradition of talking animal stories that goes back to Aesop, he has created a quiet, joyful world that readers want to return to again and again. The values of this world—a love of art, music, peace, friendship, home and nature—are ones you will want to foster in your classroom.

Reading Lobel also offers children much wisdom about being with others and being in the world. The importance of being yourself, of tolerating others, of overcoming fears, of seeing things from many points of view, of choosing flexibility rather than rigidity, are recurring motifs in his stories that children can identify with and grow from.

Finally, Lobel's skills as a storyteller and artist, his brilliant characterizations, his always present sense of humor (that is both kindhearted and very funny), and his deeply satisfying storytelling make him a wonderful author with whom to begin to an exploration of what makes great literature.

## Using This Book

This book offers many paths of entry for an Arnold Lobel study. You can use as many or as few of Lobel's books as your class needs dictate. The books can also be taught in the sequence that makes most sense to you. This book has been organized in the following way:

**Meet Arnold Lobel** This short biography of Lobel, written in language appropriate for children, is suitable for photocopying for children to refer to or for reading aloud.

**Teaching Activities for Any Time** Here you'll find ideas for activities that can be used with any Arnold Lobel book.

**Teaching With Arnold Lobel Books** This section offers in-depth explorations of Lobel's most popular books, including pre-, during-, and after-reading discussion ideas as well as activity ideas for stories in each of the books. These include features such as Author's Craft, which focuses on specific writing techniques and story structure devices used by the author—for example, the use of descriptive and repetitive language, onomatopoeia, and point of view. There are also ideas for tying all the stories in a book together and reproducible activity pages that include graphic organizers for exploring story elements, assessing students' comprehension, and more.

**Learn More With Other Arnold Lobel Books** This section treats additional Lobel books, offering activity and discussion ideas for each.

**Celebrating Arnold Lobel** Activities and discussion ideas for concluding your study.

# Getting Started With an Arnold Lobel Author Study

◎ Decide how much time you plan to spend on your author study. Will it span several weeks? Or will you study individual books in weekly intervals, spreading out your study over several months?

◎ Gather and read the books you plan to use during your study. Obtain multiple copies, if possible. Become familiar with the personalities, relationships, and conflicts of the characters in the books.

◎ Set up a display on a table or shelf on which to feature the books. On a bulletin board, post clippings of interviews, articles, and photos of the author. (Post a copy of Meet Arnold Lobel, page 6.)

◎ If possible, designate a corner of your classroom as a reading center. Add big pillows or cozy armchairs. (Children will enjoy reading in chairs that are reminiscent of the kind Arnold Lobel illustrated for Frog, Toad, and other characters to sit in.)

◎ Invite volunteers to record some of the books on tape. Place the recordings in the center, along with copies of the corresponding books.

## Connections to the Language Arts Standards

The activities found in this book will support you in meeting the following primary-grade standards as outlined by Mid-Continent Regional Educational Laboratory (MCREL), an organization that collects and synthesizes national and state K–12 standards:

### Reading

**Uses the general skills and strategies of the reading process:**

◆ Uses meaning clues (e.g., title, cover, headings, story structure, story topic) to aid comprehension and make predictions about content (e.g., action, events, character's behavior)
◆ Uses basic elements of phonetic and structural analysis to decode unknown words
◆ Understands level-appropriate sight words and vocabulary
◆ Reads aloud familiar stories, poems, and passages with fluency and expression
◆ Uses reading skills and strategies to understand and interpret a variety of literary texts

**Uses reading skills and strategies to understand a variety of literary passages and texts (e.g., folktales, fiction, fables, and poems):**

◆ Knows the basic characteristics of familiar genres
◆ Knows setting, main characters, main events, sequence, and problems in stories
◆ Knows the main ideas or theme of a story
◆ Relates stories to personal experiences

Source: *Content Knowledge: A Compendium of Standards and Benchmarks for K–12 Education* (4th ed.). Mid-Continent Research for Education and Learning, 2004.

### Writing

**Uses the general skills and strategies of the writing process:**

◆ Uses prewriting strategies to plan written work
◆ Uses strategies to draft, revise, edit, and publish written work
◆ Uses strategies to organize written work (e.g., beginning, middle, and ending; sequence of events)
◆ Writes in a variety of forms or genres (e.g., friendly letters, stories, poems, responses to literature)

**Uses the stylistic and rhetorical aspects of writing:**

◆ Uses descriptive words to convey basic ideas
◆ Uses declarative and interrogative sentences in written compositions

**Uses grammatical and mechanical conventions in written compositions:**

◆ Uses conventions of print in writing
◆ Uses complete sentences in written compositions
◆ Uses parts of speech, conventions of spelling, capitalization, and punctuation in written compositions

### Listening and Speaking

**Uses listening and speaking strategies for different purposes:**

◆ Makes contributions in class and group discussions (e.g., connects ideas and experiences with those of others)
◆ Asks and responds to questions (e.g., about the meaning of a story, or of words or ideas)

# Meet Arnold Lobel

Born: May 22, 1933, in Los Angeles, California
Died: December 4, 1987

The first time Arnold Lobel tried to draw a grasshopper, he failed miserably. He looked at what he drew and thought, *That doesn't look like a grasshopper at all; that looks like a green rabbit!* But he kept at it, drawing and redrawing his grasshopper. Finally, after much hard work, he succeeded. Today you can read about Lobel's grasshopper in the book *Grasshopper on the Road*. Yes, even the legendary Arnold Lobel failed at times. But his willingness to fail and then try again may have been the secret to his success.

Lobel was born in Los Angeles and grew up in Schenectady, New York. He recalled: "From my house the long walk to the library was downhill all the way. I would return the books I had borrowed and would quickly stock up on five new selections. Five, as I remember, was the most books that one could take out at a time."

Lobel studied fine arts in college and discovered that he had a talent for illustrating books. In 1959 he got his first break. An editor at a publishing house liked a drawing of a cricket that Lobel had made. "Can you draw a salmon?" she asked. Lobel, who had never tried to draw a salmon, fibbed and said, "Oh yes, I do it all the time!" That day he got a job: illustrating the children's book *Red Tag Comes Home*.

## Drawing Upon His Life

Lobel believed that a writer or illustrator must draw upon the events in his or her own life. Books, he said, "have to come out of the things that I, as an author, am passionately interested in." The most famous example of Lobel's using his own life as a source of ideas is the Frog and Toad books. While vacationing in Vermont, Lobel's two children returned home with a bucketful of frogs and toads they had caught. Gradually an idea formed for a book about two best friends, a frog and a toad.

## The Process of Writing

Writing, for Arnold Lobel, was much more difficult than drawing pictures. He said, "Sitting in a chair with an open notebook on my lap, waiting for nothing to happen, is not my idea of fun."

"The creation of most picture books for children is not dramatic," Lobel said in his acceptance speech for the prestigious Caldecott Medal. "It is a matter of daily, patient, single-minded effort. It is a matter of writing words on a page in a silent room."

Sadly, Arnold Lobel suffered a long illness before he died in December 1987. Yet as he battled his disease each day, he created new books—until the very end of his life.

Once, while looking at what he knew would be his last book, *The Turnaround Wind*, Arnold Lobel happily said: "I can't believe I did what I did." Many of his readers have the same reaction. It's hard to believe that one man could contribute so much.

### A Partial Bibliography of Arnold Lobel's Books:

*A Zoo for Mister Muster*, 1962

*A Holiday for Mister Muster*, 1963

*Giant John*, 1964

*Martha, the Movie Mouse*, 1966

*Small Pig*, 1969

*Frog and Toad Are Friends*, 1970

*On the Day Peter Stuyvesant Sailed Into Town*, 1971

*Mouse Tales*, 1972

*Frog and Toad Together*, 1972

*Owl at Home*, 1975

*Frog and Toad All Year*, 1976

*Mouse Soup*, 1977

*Grasshopper on the Road*, 1978

*Days With Frog and Toad*, 1979

*Fables*, 1980

*Uncle Elephant*, 1981

*Ming Lo Moves the Mountain*, 1982

*The Book of Pigericks: Pig Limericks*, 1983

### Selected Works Cocreated With Anita Lobel:

*How the Rooster Saved the Day*, 1977

*A Treeful of Pigs*, 1979

*On Market Street*, 1981

*The Rose in My Garden*, 1984

Information for "Meet Arnold Lobel" was excerpted from *The Big Book of Picture-Book Authors and Illustrators*, by James Preller (Scholastic, 2001). Copyright © 2001 by James Preller.

# Teaching Activities for Any Time

To enhance your author study, choose from this host of interdisciplinary activities that will work well with any of Arnold Lobel's books.

## Language Arts, Drama, and Art

❖ ❈ ❖

Lobel's vivid language and vibrant characters make his stories ideal for dramatization. And his wonderful prose and delightful illustrations make language arts and arts activities a natural connection for an author study. Here are few of the many possible ideas:

### Reading Chapter Books

Explore chapter books with children, focusing on the table of contents.

**Before Reading**

❋ Invite children to review a book's features by looking at the cover (see Close-Up on the Cover, right, for more), the jacket flap (or back cover), the title page, and the table of contents.

❋ Ask children to read the title of each chapter or story and share what they think it might be about.

**After Reading**

❋ Have children review the table of contents again and compare their predictions about each story or chapter with what it was really about. Now that they have read the book, the table of contents will have much more meaning than it did before.

❋ Working in groups, have children write a brief summary of what happens in each chapter or story. Have them skim the book, if necessary, to refresh their memories.

### Close-Up on the Cover

To help build children's prediction skills, examine a book's cover with them before reading. Read the title and encourage them to study the illustrations. Ask children to think about and then share what these features might indicate about the book. Then preview the book with a picture walk. As you leaf through the book, encourage children to share what they observe happening in the illustrations on each page. What new information about the book do these pictures suggest?

### Focus on Fluency

Arnold Lobel's books offer many opportunities to help children develop fluency in their reading. Model how to read the books with expression and proper phrasing. Particularly focus on how to read sentences with punctuation marks such as question marks and exclamation points, as well as how to read dialogue. Demonstrate how to emphasize print features, such as words in all capital letters or italicized words. As you reread, ask children to chime in on these words.

Since the books have short chapters or stories, they lend themselves well to paired reading. Small groups might also read the books aloud, choosing parts and reading the dialogue to one another. Place recorded tapes of your fluent readings in the listening center or class library for children to practice.

### Character Mirrors

Have children keep a running list of the endearing quirks and familiar qualities that the characters in the books have that remind children of themselves. Suggest that they choose a character whose quirks mirror their own. They can write this list on a copy of the hand mirror pattern on page 34. Have children use their character mirrors as they read the books or as story starters to write their own stories.

## Story Elements Relay Game

Write "Plot," "Character," and "Setting" on several sets of index cards. Divide the class or groups into two teams. Have one person from the first team choose a card. Then the team must describe a character, plot, or setting from one of the books, depending on the chosen card. The opposite team must then name the book. If they correctly name it, they get a point and choose a card. If not, the other team gets a point. Play continues until one team scores an agreed upon number of points.

## Summarize the Story

Have children practice summarizing stories by answering the following questions:

◎ "Who are the characters in this story?"

◎ "What is the most important thing that happens in this story?"

◎ "What surprised you most when you read this story?"

## Funny Times Book

Have children note the funny incidents in the different books. Invite them to draw their favorite scenes in comic book form. Compile these into individual or collaborative comic books.

## Arnold Lobel Word Line

String a clothesline in your Arnold Lobel corner or in one section of the classroom. On large cards, have children write key words and phrases from Arnold Lobel's books. Hang these on the clothesline with clothespins. Invite children to choose from these to make "found" poems and stories.

## Television Talk Show

Invite children to choose characters from different books to appear together on a talk show. Have them skim their favorite Arnold Lobel books and select the characters to be invited to the talk show. Suggest that they decide which character would make the best host. Invite them to brainstorm questions for the host to ask. Guest characters might think about some of their answers in advance of the show. Tape-record or videotape the show, if possible. If they like, children can act out the show with sock, paper bag, or craft stick puppets that represent the characters.

# Charts, Graphs, Maps, and Diagrams

When doing an author study, it is particularly useful for children to use graphic representations such as maps, charts, and diagrams. This can help them make generalizations, compare and contrast, and understand what makes this author stand out from others. Use some of the following ideas:

## Arnold Lobel's World

The settings in many of Arnold Lobel's books seem to take place in the same fictional world. It is a simple world inhabited by talking animals that both dress and live like humans. Help children recognize this common Lobel world by asking questions, such as "Who lives in this world? Are there cities and cars? What kinds of activities do the characters enjoy?" Make an Arnold Lobel's World chart. For each new book, check off the features that apply and add new ones.

| Arnold Lobel's World | | | |
|---|---|---|---|
| **Story Features** | **Frog and Toad Are Friends** | **Grasshopper on the Road** | **Owl at Home** |
| talking animals | ✳ | ✳ | ✳ |
| wear clothes | ✳ | ✳ | ✳ |
| live in the woods and meadow | ✳ | ✳ | ✳ |
| eat "people" food | ✳ | ✳ | ✳ |
| live in little houses | ✳ | ✳ | ✳ |
| no cars, big buildings, or cities | ✳ | ✳ | ✳ |

## Biography Chart

Have children refer to the Arnold Lobel biography on page 6 or additional resources. Ask them to make a list of several key events in his life. Then invite children to skim Arnold Lobel books and find events or characters that relate to his life. Help them put this information into chart form.

## Giant Venn

Use yarn or string to make a large Venn diagram with two or more overlapping circles on the floor of the classroom. Label each circle with the name of one of Arnold Lobel's books. On index cards, have children write down features of each of the books. Then have them place the cards on the diagram, putting features that the books have in common into the overlapping areas. You may want to circulate to help children identify where the cards should go and discuss changes, if necessary.

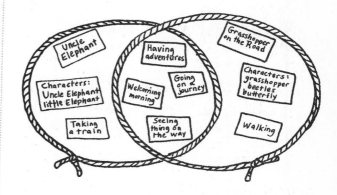

## Happy/Sad Bar Graph

Have children draw or photocopy illustrations (reducing them if you have this feature available) that show happy and sad moments in the stories. As a group, make a large bar graph, compiling the happy moments on one bar and the sad ones on another. Then discuss what information we learn about Arnold Lobel's books from this graph.

## Arnold Lobel's World Map

Use a large sheet from a roll of wrapping paper or several pieces of posterboard taped together to form the background for a large map. Invite children to draw elements of their favorite stories on areas of the map, such as Frog's house and Grasshopper's road. Let children take turns contributing to the map.

# Owl at Home

◆ ❋ ◆

## (HARPERCOLLINS, 1975)

**L**ife at Owl's cozy home inside the tree is rarely quiet. And Owl himself is usually the source of the commotion. Whether letting in a winter storm because he thinks it's a guest, chasing himself up and down the stairs because he wants to be in two places at once, or thinking of sad things to make tear-water tea, there is always something going on.

### Threading Through the Book

## Owl Is Funny Chart (Exploring Character)

One of the most fruitful ways of connecting the individual stories in *Owl at Home* is to focus on their humor and how that relates to the character Owl. In many ways, Owl is like a young child who sees himself as the center of the universe and who believes that inanimate objects are as alive with thoughts and feelings as he himself is—at one moment thinking that the moon is following him because it wants to be his friend, at another being terrified of the strange bumps at the end of his bed (really his own feet).

This element of Owl's character is the starting point for the story plots and is at the heart of what makes them funny. Keep an ongoing Owl Is Funny chart, such as the one below, that you can fill in after you finish each story. Help children identify that the funny part of each story involves the childlike way in which Owl is looking at the world around him.

### Owl Is Funny

| Story | What Owl Thinks | What Happens | What Is Funny |
|---|---|---|---|
| **The Guest** | Winter is a guest that wants to come in. | He lets it in and it takes over the whole house. | Owl treats winter as if it were a person. |
| **Strange Bumps** | He sees strange bumps at the bottom of his bed. | He tries to see and get away from the bumps. | The bumps are really his own feet. |

## Connecting to Other Arnold Lobel Books

◆ ❋ ◆

**O**wl at Home has the humor, characterization, and pastoral setting found in much of Lobel's work. Owl is like the more well-known Toad (of the Frog and Toad books), who has a similarly childlike way of looking at the world and of working himself up into a humorous hysteria when it doesn't conform to his ideas. Unlike other Lobel books, in which there are additional characters that represent a more adult point of view (such as Frog), in the Owl stories, Owl is always alone. When reading subsequent Lobel books, it may be helpful to ask children how a certain character reminds them of Owl.

# "The Guest"

## Before Reading

Ask children if they have ever listened to storms when they are indoors. What sounds do they hear? Have they ever imagined that the storm sounds are something else? Explain that they are going to read about an owl that is listening to a storm.

## During Reading

Encourage children to predict what the storm will do once it gets inside Owl's home and how Owl will get rid of it. Ask them what is funny about the way Owl treats winter. Help children recognize that Owl is treating winter as if it were a person.

## After Reading

After reading the last page, ask children what they think of the way Owl got rid of winter. Do they think this could really happen? Why or why not?

## Author's Craft

### Vivid Verbs
(Using Descriptive Language)

Help children recognize the descriptive verbs Lobel uses to make the commotion in Owl's house come alive. Point out the way the storm is "banging and pounding" and "knocking and thumping" at the door, the way it makes the window shades "flap and shiver," or the way the wind "whirled" and "whooshed."

Have children think of other vivid verbs that describe the commotion in Owl's house. Brainstorm a list of other words that describe a storm as well. Record these on a word wall. Then invite children to draw a picture of a storm and write about it, using at least three vivid verbs.

## Extending the Story

### Make a Character Web
(Identifying Character Traits)

Ask children what they can tell about Owl from this story: "What did Owl do that made the story funny? What did Owl think or do that you wouldn't think or do?"

Find instances of Owl's speaking, and read them aloud together. What does each tell about Owl? For example, when Owl invites the winter in to warm itself, elicit that this suggests Owl is kindhearted and friendly. Begin a character web such as the one below. Add to the web as you continue to read the stories.

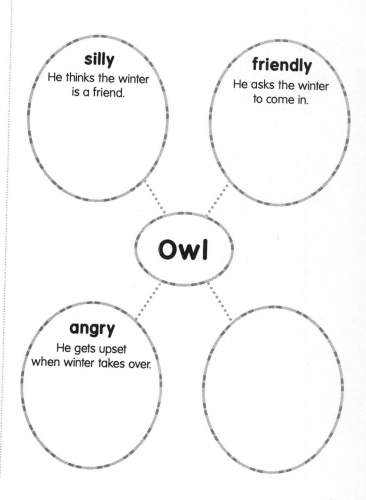

**silly**
He thinks the winter is a friend.

**friendly**
He asks the winter to come in.

**Owl**

**angry**
He gets upset when winter takes over.

# "Strange Bumps"

## Before Reading

Ask children if they ever imagine they see strange things in the dark. When they turned on the lights, what did these imaginary things turn out to be? Tell them that in the story they are about to read, Owl sees something odd at the foot of his bed. Ask what they think that might be.

## During Reading

The story never once states that the bumps at the foot of Owl's bed are really his own feet. However, children should be able to infer this using the pictures and common sense. Ask children how they could tell what the bumps were. Have them suggest ways that Owl might have been able to figure it out, too.

## After Reading

If you are keeping the Owl Is Funny chart (page 10), now is a good time to begin making connections. If not, simply ask children how Owl's behavior in this story is similar to his behavior in "The Guest." Help children see that in the first story, Owl thought he was hearing something he wasn't (the winter asking to come in), and in the second story Owl thought he was seeing something he wasn't (bumps instead of feet).

## Extending the Story

### Write a New Ending (Exploring Problems and Solutions)

Point out that the plot of many books and stories centers on a character who has a problem that he or she must solve. Ask children what the problem is in "Strange Bumps." In what way does Owl attempt to solve it? Fill out a problem/solution chart for the story, like the one below.

Ask children to think of a different ending to the story. Have them write or tell their new endings.

| Problem | How He Tries to Solve It | How He Does Solve It |
|---|---|---|
| Owl thinks he sees strange bumps at the bottom of his bed. | He tries to find out what the bumps are by removing his covers, but all he sees are his feet. | He decides to sleep downstairs. |

## What Do I See in the Dark?
(Poetry)

Extend your Before Reading discussion by sharing the following poem with children. Copy the poem onto chart paper and read it aloud. Then read it again, asking children to read along with you. Afterward, invite children to write their own poems about strange things they've imagined seeing in the dark. If they like, children might innovate on the structure of this poem, substituting their own imaginary things.

### What Do I See in the Dark?

What do I see in the dark?
Is it a bear?
A big, big bear?

What do I see in the dark?
Is it a horse?
A tall, tall horse?

What do I see in the dark?
Is it a bat?
A small, small bat?

There is no big, big bear.
That is my coat on a chair.

There is no tall, tall horse.
That is my dresser, of course!

There is no small, small bat.
That is an old party hat.

I see no bat, horse, or bear.
But what is that over there?

—Kathleen M. Hollenbeck

# "Tear-Water Tea"

## Before Reading

Tell children that in the story they are going to read, Owl tries to make tea from tears. What kinds of things do they think Owl would think of to make himself cry? What might they think about if they wanted to make themselves cry?

## During Reading

As they read, help children notice that the things Owl cries about are all things that can no longer be used or are no longer appreciated. Ask, "In what ways are these things the same?" Once they have recognized this pattern, invite children to predict other things that Owl will think of to make himself cry.

## After Reading

Ask children if they ever feel sad when something is not used or appreciated. How does this story add to their understanding of Owl's character? Have them add to the character web (page 11).

## Extending the Story

### Tear-Water Teapots
(Critical Thinking, Writing)

Talk about the different ways the things in "Tear-Water Tea" are no longer useful or appreciated. Some things are lost, some things are broken, and some things people just aren't interested in anymore. Then invite children to fill their own tear-water teapots.

**1.** Provide each child with a copy of the teapot, lid, and teardrop patterns on page 16. Invite them to color and cut out the patterns.

**2.** On each tear, have them write one thing that is no longer used or appreciated and tell why.

**3.** To assemble their teapots, children apply a glue stick around the outer edges of the teapot only and attach it to a sheet of construction paper.

**4.** Next, they secure the lid to the teapot with a brass fastener. Students can then lift the lid to deposit their tears.

Invite children to share the tears in their tear-water teapots with one another.

# "Upstairs and Downstairs"

## Before Reading

Ask children to name two favorite places in their homes. Have they ever wanted to be in both places at once? Tell them that in the story they are about to read, Owl has a problem. He wants to be upstairs and downstairs at the same time. How do they think he will solve this problem?

## During Reading

If you are reading the story aloud, model for children how expression adds to the story. Exaggerate the humor by making your voice more and more frantic as Owl runs up and down the stairs. Ask children whether they think Owl will ever solve this problem. What might he do?

## After Reading

Ask children what they think about the story's ending. Do they think of Owl's solution as a solution? Why or why not? How might Owl have altered his expectations so that he could enjoy both places in his home?

## Extending the Story

### In the Middle (Math, Art)

Owl solves his problem of wanting to be both upstairs and downstairs by sitting on the middle step—or the tenth step out of 20. Invite children to discover if this is really the middle step. Together, count 20 craft sticks or other manipulatives and lay them one above the other, like stairs. Then pull out slightly the tenth one from the bottom. Have children count the sticks before the tenth and after. Are there the same number of objects? (*no*) Guide children to recognize that when there is an even number of objects, there is no exact middle.

Have children explore finding the middle in other series of objects. Suggest some odd and some even numbers. Encourage children to recognize that some numbers have a "middle" object (the odd numbers) and others don't.

Invite children to draw any number of steps. Have them find the middle and draw a picture of Owl. Is Owl halfway between two steps or on a step?

## Author's Craft

### Create a Conversation (Using Dialogue)

Have children notice the way Owl talks to himself as if he were another person. Read the dialogue together. Point out the repetitive language and the way Owl always addresses himself by name. Invite children to have fun making up dialogue for themselves. Have them think of a funny situation like Owl's, in which they are trying to do two things at the same time. Or they can think of a choice or decision in which one side wants to do one thing and the other side wants to do another. Invite children to write or perform their dialogues.

# "Owl and the Moon"

## Before Reading

Talk about the moon. Ask children to share what they have noticed about the moon. Is the moon always the same size and shape? What color is it? Have they ever seen the moon during the day?

## During Reading

Ask, "Why does Owl think he and the moon must be good friends?" and "Why does he feel sad when the moon disappears?"

## After Reading

Ask children how this story is similar to the first story in the book, "The Guest." Guide children to infer that in both stories, Owl thinks that a "thing" in nature wants to be his friend. In both stories he begins to feel overwhelmed by his new "friend" and wants to be rid of it. However, in the last story, Owl has been able to put enough distance between himself and his new friend to want to remain friends.

## Extending the Story

### Why the Moon Follows Me (Science)

Help children understand why the moon seems to be following Owl. Point out that the reason is that the moon is so far away. (If you could drive to the moon on a highway, it would take almost five months!) Invite children to perform the following activity that demonstrates how the distance of an object can cause the "following me" effect.

◎ Have children line up two chairs. One chair should be placed four or five yards behind the other.

◎ Then have children walk past the chairs (moving perpendicular to the line of the two chairs) as they look directly over their shoulder. They should see the farther chair for longer.

Explain that since the moon is so very far away, you see it no matter how far you walk or drive, so it looks like it is following you.

## Author's Craft

## Setting Theater (Exploring Setting)

Help children review the settings in this story by doing a retelling. Let children create simple cutout puppets of Owl and the moon from tagboard or construction paper. Have them attach craft sticks to both. Ask children where Owl is in the beginning of the story (the sea), in the middle of the story (the woods), and at the end of the story (at home). Have them use a single piece of tagboard and divide it into three sections. Invite children to draw these three settings on the tagboard. Then display the settings on a chalkboard ledge. Children can crouch down to retell the story using the settings and the two puppets.

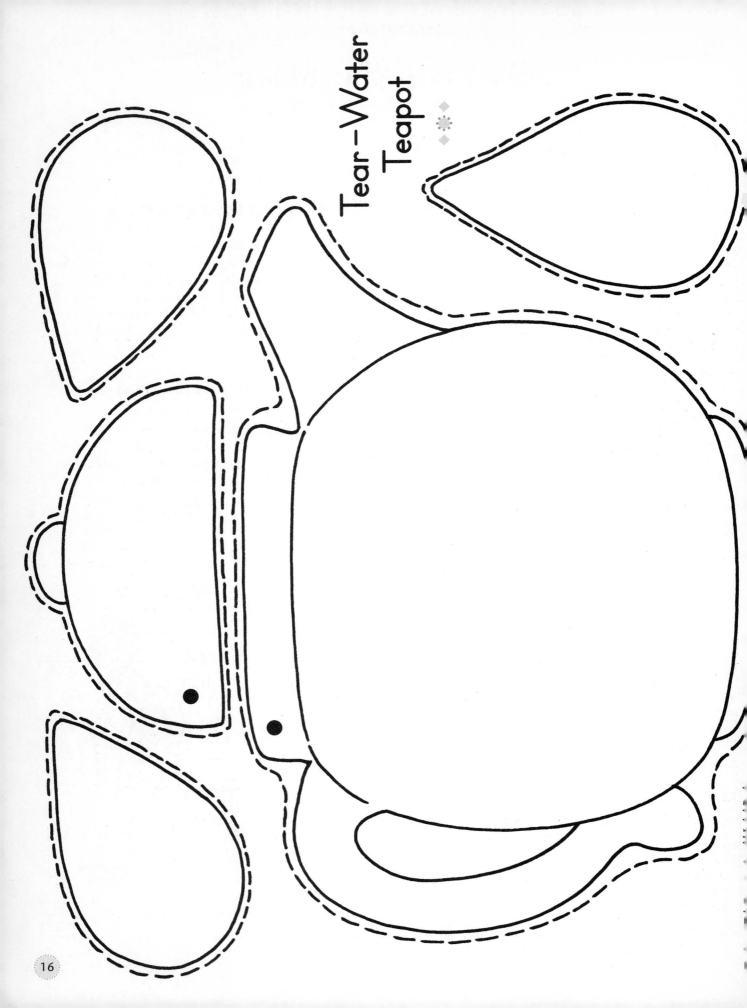

Tear–Water Teapot

# Tying It All Together

## Compare and Contrast Stories
(Building Reading Comprehension)

Ask children which Owl stories were their favorites. Invite them to find connections between the stories by asking questions such as the following:

✳ "In which stories is Owl silly? Are there any stories in which Owl isn't silly?"

✳ "In which stories does Owl think something has feelings that doesn't?"

✳ "In which stories does Owl want to do things that can't be done?"

✳ "In which stories did you feel bad for Owl or worried about him?"

✳ "Would you want to be Owl's friend? Why or why not?"

## Write a New Owl Story (Writing)

Invite children to write a new Owl story using their own Owl-like experiences. Point out that many of Owl's silly ideas are the kinds of ideas that children themselves might have now or have had when they were younger. Brainstorm ideas by asking:

✳ "Did you ever see something in the dark? What did you think it was? What did it really turn out to be?"

✳ "Did you ever want to be friends with something that couldn't talk, like a plant or a toy or the moon? What did you wish it would say?"

✳ "Did you ever try to make yourself scared or sad? What did you do or think of? What happened?"

Children can either pick one idea to work on as a group or work on their own. Fill in a story chart such as the one below. Point out that even though these ideas might come from real-life experiences, they can shape them to make a story. Owl usually believes in a silly idea much longer than they themselves would, and that's when so many funny things happen!

| Silly Idea | What Happens First | What Happens Next | What Happens Last |
|---|---|---|---|
| Owl wanted to be friends with a flower. | He talks to the flower, but it doesn't talk back. | He gets mad at the flower. | The flower blooms and Owl thinks it is smiling and is happy. |

## Story Sequence Stairs
(Retelling and Sequencing)

Help children practice retelling and sequencing skills using the stairway in Owl's house as a graphic organizer. Give each child a sheet of 11- by 17-inch paper. Then have children follow these directions:

1. Fold the paper in half the short way, and then in half two more times.

2. Unfold the paper and refold it like a fan. Then unfold the paper again.

3. Number the "stairs" First, Second, Third, and Last —one for each of the main events in a story.

Have children choose one of the stories in *Owl at Home* to retell. Direct them to write the title on the bottom panel. Have children then review the main events of the story and summarize and write about these events on the stairs, from the bottom stair to the top. They can draw pictures, too, if they like.

Then invite each child to draw and cut out a small picture of Owl. Have children pair up and let Owl climb the stairs as they retell the stories to each other.

## Exploring Character

Assess children's understanding of Owl's characteristics using the activity on page 18.

Activity Page

Name ______________________________ Date ____________________

# The Many Sides of Owl

Each of the sentences below tells what Owl is like. Read each one and then write about a time Owl acted that way. Draw a picture to show Owl acting in that way, too.

**Owl is nice.**

He ______________________________

______________________________.

**Owl is silly.**

He ______________________________

______________________________.

**Owl is nervous.**

He ______________________________

______________________________.

**Now you tell what Owl is like!**

Owl is ______________________________.

He ______________________________.

# Frog and Toad Are Friends

◆❋◆

(HARPERCOLLINS, 1970)

**F**rog and Toad Are Friends is the first of four books in this hugely popular series. Like many Lobel books, the Frog and Toad stories relate the small joys and pains in the daily lives of animal characters. An important part of the series' lasting appeal is the way that it captures a very special friendship. These stories will give children the chance to focus on their own experiences with friendship. They will also introduce children to two hilarious, highly endearing, and very human amphibians that they will want to know better.

## Threading Through the Book

## Frog and Toad Are Different Chart

(Comparing and Contrasting Characters)

Frog and Toad may be best friends, but they have very different personalities. While Frog is easy-going and uncomplicated, enjoying each moment as it comes, Toad is often anxious and has a way of making life difficult for himself.

It is interesting to think about how the personalities of Frog and Toad in some ways suggest the animals they are: Frogs are more graceful, easy-moving, and seem less affected by the weight of the world, much like the character of Frog. Toads are wartier and have a more comical and stubborn appearance, much like the character of Toad.

Help children recognize these and other differences by creating a Frog and Toad Are Different chart. First, record two or three things each character did in a given story. Then brainstorm words that describe each character's behavior. As your chart develops, underline similar words and phrases that appear under each character's name and talk about whether these characteristics appear in the other stories.

### Frog and Toad Are Different

| Story | What Frog Does | What Frog Is Like | What Toad Does | What Toad Is Like |
|-------|----------------|-------------------|----------------|-------------------|
| **Spring** | • shouts because he is excited about spring <br> • tricks Toad at the end | • likes to have fun <br> • smart, tricky | • doesn't want to get out of bed <br> • gets tricked by Frog | • cranky, stubborn <br> • doesn't always think, can be fooled |
| **The Story** | • tells about Toad's story at the end | • thoughtful <br> • smart, good at thinking of things | • tries crazy things to think of a story | • will do a lot for a friend, tries too hard, gets worried |

## Connecting to Other Arnold Lobel Books

◆❋◆

**F**rog and Toad represent two common Lobel character types—the calmer and more integrated character, Frog, (also exemplified by Grasshopper or Uncle Elephant) and the more childlike, anxious, and comical character, Toad, (represented by Owl and nearly all the characters Grasshopper meets on his journey). Connect the books by asking questions, such as:

✳ "Who does Owl remind you more of, Frog or Toad? Who do you think Owl would be better friends with?"

✳ "What might Frog do or say to Owl when he wants to be both upstairs and downstairs? What do you think Toad would do or say?"

✳ "Which character do you think would go on the road like Grasshopper, Frog or Toad?"

# "Spring"

## Before Reading

Ask children what they like about spring. How do they feel in spring? Explain that children are going to read about how two friends, Frog and Toad, greet the spring.

## During Reading

Encourage children to identify with the situation of both characters. Have they ever been in the mood for fun while a friend wasn't? Have they ever been tired or in a bad mood when a friend wanted to play? What would they do if they were Frog and wanted to get Toad out of bed?

## After Reading

✳ Talk about the ending with students. Discuss how Frog tricks Toad into getting out of bed in the end. Ask, "Is that an okay kind of trick to play?"

✳ Reinforce calendar skills. Display a calendar and ask students to name the month and season in which Frog first fell asleep. In which month and season did Frog want to wake up? If he had really slept all that time, how many months would that have been? Which season would he have slept though?

## Author's Craft

# What We Can Do Poems
### (Using Action Words)

Reread the section of the story in which Frog recites: "We will skip through the meadow and run through the woods and swim in the river. And in the evenings we will sit right here on the porch and count the stars." Point out that each thing Frog wants to do is represented by a different action word. He also tells where he would like to do each thing.

Brainstorm things that children like to do with their friends. Then invite them to write a poem telling five things they like to do with a friend. Encourage them to use a different action word for each activity and to add details that tell how, where, or when they would like to do the activity.

## Extending the Story

## Who Hibernates? Lift-and-Look
(Science)

Ask children why Toad had been asleep since November. Talk about hibernation. Explain that when animals hibernate, they go into a sleeplike state. Their body temperatures drop and their heart and breathing rates slow down. Why do children think that animals hibernate during the winter? (*lower temperatures, limited food available*) Tell them that both frogs and toads are deep hibernators. Then invite children to get a close-up look at other animal hibernators. Give each child a copy of pages 25–26. Then have them follow these steps to make the manipulative:

**1.** Cut along the outer dotted lines on each page.

**2.** Cut open the seven flaps along the dotted lines on page 25.

**3.** Apply a glue stick around the edges of page 26.

**4.** Place page 25 on top of page 26, line up the corners, and then seal by pressing the pages together.

**5.** Invite children to lift the flaps to read and learn about different animals that hibernate.

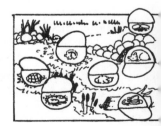

### My Friend and I

We tell funny stories on the couch.
We play soccer in the park after school.
We bake yummy cookies in the kitchen.
We ride our bikes to the store.
We build a great big snowman in my yard.

# "The Story"

## Before Reading

Ask children if they like to make up stories. Where do they get their ideas? What would they do if they had to think of a story but couldn't? Where would they look for an idea?

## During Reading

Ask children what is funny about the way Toad is trying to think of a story. Why do they think he is getting so upset? Why might Toad think that banging his head against a wall or jumping up and down or pouring water over himself would help him come up with a story?

## After Reading

❋ Talk about Frog and Toad's friendship. Ask, "How is Toad acting like a good friend in this story? How is Frog acting like a good friend?" Why do children think Frog chose to tell the story about Toad at the end?

❋ Ask children how Toad is acting the same as he did in "Spring." (*In both stories, Toad gets upset in a funny way.*) What new dimension of his character do they see in this story? How is Frog acting the same?

## Author's Craft

### Frog and Toad Talk
#### (Exploring Conventions of Dialogue)

Point out the repetitive dialogue Lobel uses each time Toad does something to think of a story.

**"Why are you _____?" asked Frog.**

**"I hope that if I _____, it will help me to think of a story," said Toad.**

Write the sentence frames above on the board but leave out the quotation marks. Invite children to add them. Explain that these marks tell when someone is speaking. Have children think of other silly things Toad could do to help him think of a story. Create new sentences using these ideas and insert quotation marks and other punctuation. You can also use them for the Silly Scene Movie Screens activity, right.

## Extending the Story

### Silly Scene Movie Screens
(Oral Language, Art)

Ask children to think of three new silly things Toad could do to think of a story. Have them make a "movie" of these three things by doing the following:

1. Center a sheet of 8 1/2- by 11-inch paper horizontally on an open file folder. Then trace it.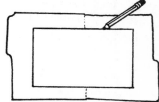

2. Remove the paper and fold the file folder in half lenghthwise, with the traced outline facing out.

3. Starting at the folded edge, make two cuts along the traced lines. Then open the folder.

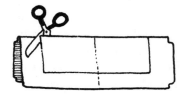

4. Have children tape together five sheets of 8 1/2- by 11-inch paper horizontally.

5. On each of the three middle sheets of paper, invite children to draw a new funny way for Toad to think of a story.

6. Help children thread their scenes through their screens. (Make the slits deeper, if needed.) Then invite children to show and tell about their new scenes by pulling the paper through. Encourage them to use Frog's and Toad's repetitive phrases from the story (see Author's Craft, left).

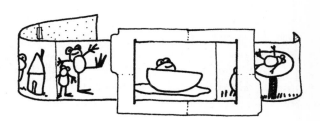

# "A Lost Button"

### Before Reading

Ask children if they have ever lost anything. Did they try to look for it? Did they ever find it? Tell children they will be reading a story about a lost button. Why might a button be hard to find?

### During Reading

* After Frog and Toad have found two buttons, ask children if they notice a pattern in the story. What is wrong with the first button? What is wrong with the second button? What other things do they think will be wrong with the buttons?

* After Toad finds the button at home, stop and ask what children think he will do.

### After Reading

Ask children how Toad reacted to Frog's offer of help. Ask, "How would you have felt if you were Frog? What does this tell you about what Toad is like? What does it tell you about Frog?" Add children's responses to your Frog and Toad Are Different chart (page 19).

### Extending the Story

## Button Sort (Math)

Ask children to identify the button features that helped Toad know that he had found the wrong button (color, number of holes, shape, size, thickness). Then prepare the following activity for children to do in groups. For each group, fill a resealable plastic bag with ten buttons of varying attributes.

Give each group a bag. Tell each group to pick out one button to be Toad's button. Have the group write a set of characteristics that distinguish it from the other buttons in the bag. Have each group glue their buttons onto the top half of a sheet of posterboard and write the characteristics below. Then ask each group to share their collection with the class and read the characteristics of their group's button. Challenge the rest of the class to guess which of that group's buttons is Toad's.

### Author's Craft

## The Language of Feelings
### (Using Descriptive Language)

Talk about the way Lobel shows Toad getting more and more upset as he looks for his buttons. Point out that one way you can tell Toad is upset is by the words that follow the quotation marks when he speaks (*cried Toad, wailed Toad, shouted Toad*).

Brainstorm other words that can be used to tell how someone is saying something (*sighed, laughed, yelled, whispered, squealed, asked*).

Then have children cut out pictures from magazines of people in different moods doing different things. Have them paste the picture onto a sheet of paper and write a sentence of dialogue that the person in the picture might say. Encourage students to use a word that shows feelings after the quotation marks. Make a bulletin board display entitled "Say It With Feelings," and display children's work.

Our button is round.
Our button has no dots.
Our button is not green or purple.
Our button has 4 holes.
Our button is not all one color.
Find our button.

Group 2. Luis, Angela, Matt, Ellen

# "A Swim"

## Before Reading

Talk about being embarrassed. Ask children what kinds of things make them embarrassed. How do they feel when they are embarrassed? What has helped them to stop feeling this way?

## During Reading

As you read, ask children if they have ever felt like Toad does. Do they think Toad will really look funny in his bathing suit, or does he just think he will look funny? Point out that none of the other animals wear bathing suits. Ask, "What about Toad's personality might make him want to wear a bathing suit?"

## After Reading

Ask children if they were surprised that Toad did, in fact, turn out to look silly in his bathing suit. Were they surprised that the other animals laughed at him? Ask, "What would have been another, more typical story ending?" Do children think this ending is better? Why or why not? What do they think Toad is feeling at the end?

## Extending the Story

### I Get Embarrassed When . . .
(Writing, Personal Development)

Invite children to write and illustrate pages about what makes them embarrassed. With children's permission, display the drawings on a bulletin board. Then compare notes on embarrassment. Do children get embarrassed over similar things? Do they wish they didn't feel that way? Guide children to help each other share their embarrassments and perhaps get over them a little.

## River Critter Characteristics
(Science)

In "A Swim," children meet a variety of animals that live in and around a river. Help them sharpen their classification skills by comparing and contrasting the characteristics of these animals. Give each child a copy of page 27.

Have children cut apart the animal cards. (Besides the animals named in the story, a few additional animals common to a river habitat have been added.) Then ask them to describe characteristics of the different animals. How are they alike and different?

Next, challenge children to think of ways to group the animals. For example, animals with legs and animals without legs. Have children continue sorting their animals into two groups using other characteristics.

Encourage children to keep a record of the different groups they make. Afterward, have the class come together to share results.

# "The Letter"

## Before Reading

Talk about children's experiences with mail. How do they feel when they get mail? Have they ever waited for a letter or package to come? Invite them to describe their feelings.

## During Reading

As you read, talk about how Toad is feeling. Have children ever felt that way? Also ask:

* "Why is a snail a funny animal to be a letter carrier?"
* "Why did Frog decide to tell Toad about the letter before he got it?"

## After Reading

What do children think of the way Frog told Toad about the letter before he received it? Do they think this was a good thing to do? Why is this a better ending than if Frog had not told Toad? Why would the other ending have been better?

## Extending the Story

### Snail Mail (Writing)

Use this story as a springboard for helping students practice writing a friendly letter. Give children shoe boxes to use as mailboxes at their desks. Have them decorate their boxes and write their names on them. Then write children's names on a sheet of paper and designate a pen pal for each. Invite children to write a friendly letter to their pen pal telling something about themselves and what they would like to do together as friends.

Then have them fold up their letter and seal closed using a glue stick and a copy of the snail pattern, below.

Tell children to try to "sneak" the letter into their pen pal's box during the day.

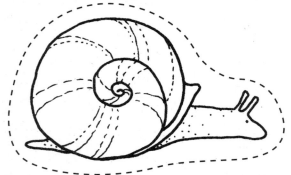

**snail pattern**

### Window Talk (Retelling, Drama)

In the story, Frog repeatedly looks out the window, anticipating the snail's arrival. Finally, Toad joins him there and they look out the window together. Invite children to reenact the story by making simple craft stick puppets of Frog and Toad. Create this window frame "stage" for them to perform behind.

1. Fold a piece of cardboard, about 12 by 18 inches, in half the short way.

2. Starting at the folded edge, make two cuts about six inches deep, as shown.

3. Cut open the folded section as shown.

4. Open the cardboard and fold back the cut pieces to create shutters. Decorate as desired. (Place a bubble of tape behind the shutters to hold them open, if needed.)

5. Tape the window frame stage to a desk or table.

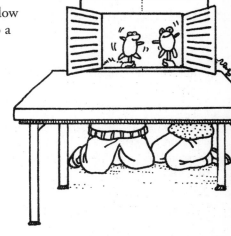

# Who Hibernates? Lift-and-Look

**Top Page**

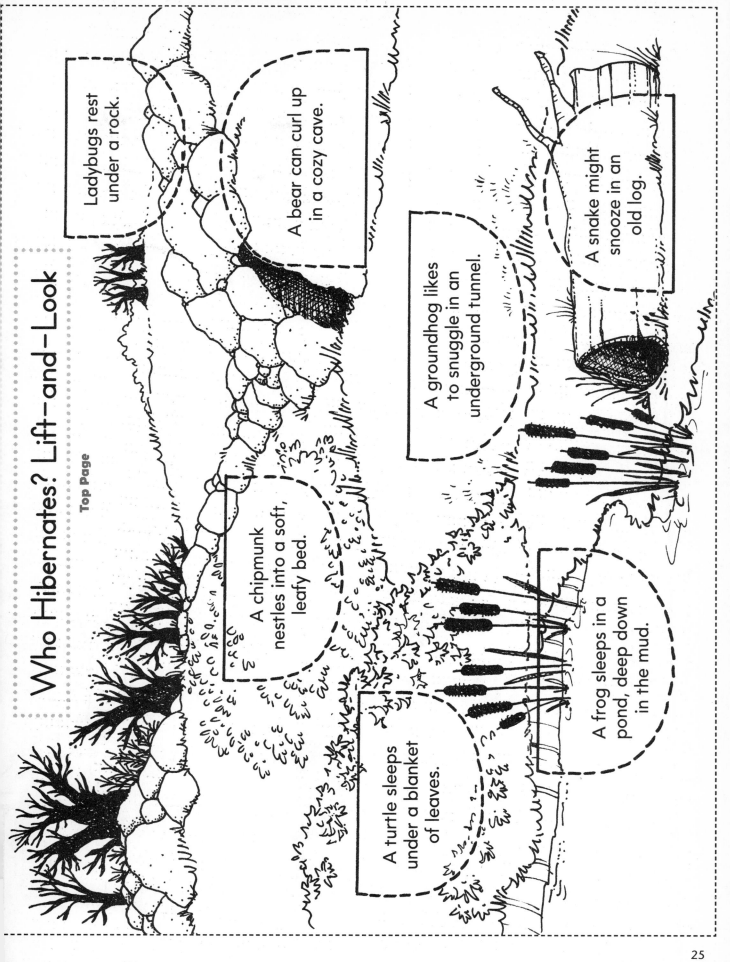

Ladybugs rest under a rock.

A bear can curl up in a cozy cave.

A snake might snooze in an old log.

A groundhog likes to snuggle in an underground tunnel.

A chipmunk nestles into a soft, leafy bed.

A turtle sleeps under a blanket of leaves.

A frog sleeps in a pond, deep down in the mud.

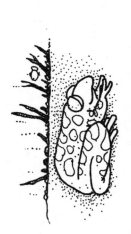

## Who Hibernates? Lift–and–Look

**Bottom Page**

dragonfly

frog

wood duck

turtle

beaver

fish

heron

water bug

snake

newt

snail

muskrat

# Frog and Toad Together

❖❋❖

(HARPERCOLLINS, 1972)

**F**rog and Toad Together features five more sweet and funny stories about these lovable and quirky best friends. When Toad makes a list of things to do that day, Frog helps him follow it. When Toad bakes cookies, neither he nor Frog can stop eating them. And when both Frog and Toad are scared, they are brave together. Children who have read the other Frog and Toad books will immediately recognize the same affectionately portrayed foibles, the humor, and the sweet, simple stories. Children who are new to the series will find Frog and Toad Together a wonderful place to begin.

## Threading Through the Book

### Who and What Starts It Chart (Exploring Story Structure)

**Note**

▲▲▲▲▲▲

If you haven't read Frog and Toad Are Friends, you may want to replace or augment this chart with the Frog and Toad Are Different chart on page 19.

Because of their simplicity, the Frog and Toad stories offer a wonderful opportunity to explore story structure. These stories combine character and plot in a special way. Most follow a cause-and-effect story structure, with Toad the worrywart acting as the instigator and Frog often acting as the character who can bring closure to the situation. Help children think about how these stories are structured by creating a Who and What Starts It chart such as the one below.

### Who and What Starts It

| Story | Who and What Starts It | What Happens Next | How It Ends |
|---|---|---|---|
| **A List** | Toad makes a list of all the things he will do that day. | He loses the list and can't do anything until he finds it. | Frog tells Toad to go to sleep, and Toad realizes that was the last thing on his list. |
| **The Garden** | Toad wants to make a garden. | He gets worried that the plants won't grow and does funny things to help them. | The plants grow anyway, but not because of the things Toad does. |
| **Cookies** | Toad makes cookies. | He and Frog can't stop eating them. | They give the cookies away. Frog is proud. Toad is sad. |

After you have filled in a few stories, talk about the similarities you find. Why do children think that Toad is so often the one who "starts it?" How does that make sense given his personality? How does Frog help Toad? Have children note that taking something to an extreme (for example, eating all the cookies, not being able to do anything without the list, working overtime to make the plants feel comfortable) is often what moves the story forward.

# "A List"

## Before Reading

Talk with children about the different kinds of lists people make. Why do people make lists? Have children ever made a list? What was on it? If they were going to list everything they were supposed to do today, what would be the last thing on the list?

## During Reading

Ask children what is funny about the kinds of things Toad is putting on his list. (*They aren't usually the kinds of things one needs to remember to do.*) Have them predict some other things he might add to his list. What might be the last thing on Toad's list?

## After Reading

Focus on Frog's role in the story:

❋ What do children think Frog thinks about the list?

❋ Does Frog really think it is as wonderful as he says?

❋ How does Frog show he is a good friend to Toad in this story? Talk about how being a good friend can mean that you help and support someone in what he or she wants to do, even if it is not the kind of thing you want to do.

## Extending the Story

### Make a List (Writing)

Make a list of all the things the class will do today. Invite children to include simple, ordinary things such as those that appear on Toad's list. For example, in addition to class activities, they could include individual activities such as putting their coats on for recess. As the day progresses, have children cross off each item on the list.

## Author's Craft

# What Are They Thinking? Bulletin Board

## (Exploring Story Structure)

Point out that Frog and Toad play very different roles in this story. Even though they are experiencing the same events, they may think and feel differently about them. Talk about what these different thoughts and feelings might be.

**1.** To make a point-of-view bulletin board, give each child two sheets of 8 1/2- by 11-inch paper.

**2.** Have children pick an event in the story that both characters participate in and draw a picture of each character on separate sheets of paper.

**3.** Direct them to add a thought balloon above each character, telling what that character is thinking and feeling. Encourage children to give the characters thoughts and feelings that aren't included in the actual text.

Display the pictures in the appropriate column on the bulletin board, and talk about the different points of view represented.

# "The Garden"

## Before Reading

Have children share their experiences with gardens and growing things. Ask, "What can we do to help a seed grow?" Make a list of their ideas.

Then tell children that in this story, Toad is waiting for his seeds to grow. Invite them to talk about times they have had to wait for something to happen. How did waiting make them feel? What kinds of things did they do to pass the time?

## During Reading

Focus on the humor in Toad's yelling at the plants to grow. Invite children to shout out the line as Toad might. What do children think will happen once Toad falls asleep?

## After Reading

Then ask children to name some of the things Toad did to help his seeds grow (*read them stories and poems, sang to then, played music*). Do children think these things really helped? Revisit the list of ideas children made before reading the story. Which things really did help Toad's seeds grow? (*soil, sun, rain, time*)

## Extending the Story

### Flower Feelings (Building Vocabulary)

Remind children that Toad thought the flowers were too scared to come out of the ground. Brainstorm a list of emotions that the flower might feel, such as scared, eager, happy, delighted, angry, lonely, sad, and embarrassed. Have children pretend to be flowers expressing each emotion as they emerge from the ground.

## Eggshell Garden (Science)

Invite children to create a garden like Toad's, using egg cartons, eggshells, and sunflower seeds. Help them note what makes their garden grow. Encourage children to connect to the story by taking turns reading, singing, and talking to the plants!

**1.** Fill eggshell halves with soil (2/3 full).

**2.** Plant a sunflower seed in each eggshell (about 1/4-inch deep).

**3.** Place the eggshells in their containers and water to moisten the soil.

**4.** Place the egg cartons in a dark spot in the room. Keep the soil moist, and check daily for sprouting plants. Have children record their observations by writing and drawing pictures in science journals.

**5.** When the seeds sprout, move the cartons to a sunny spot and continue to observe. Later on, you can transfer your plants to an outdoor garden.

# "Cookies"

## Before Reading

Ask children what willpower is. Have they ever tried to use willpower? What happened? What kinds of things do people need to use willpower for?

## During Reading

As you read, emphasize the difference between what Frog and Toad say they want to do and what they end up really doing. Invite children to pantomime eating another cookie when Frog and Toad do. Then ask,

✳ "Why do Frog and Toad continue to eat even though they say that they want to stop eating?"

✳ "Do you think Frog and Toad are helping each other use willpower or not?"

## After Reading

✳ Talk about the ending to this story. It presents two different resolutions to the willpower problem. Toad is sad that there are no more cookies to eat, and Frog is happy that he has finally shown willpower. Which point of view do children sympathize with most?

✳ How else might Frog and Toad try to avoid eating the cookies? Invite pairs of children to act out these new ideas.

## Extending the Story

## Math Picture Stories
(Math, Writing, Art)

Have children create math picture stories, using Frog and Toad's cookie eating as inspiration.

**1.** Direct children to fold a sheet of 11- by 17-inch paper into four or eight panels. On the first panel, have them begin the story by writing and illustrating the following: "Toad baked ten cookies and put them in a jar."

**2.** On each panel, tell them to add a new numerical event relating to the cookies. For example, Frog or Toad might eat one or more cookies. Or they might add new cookies to the jar. (See the sample below.)

**3.** On the last panel, have them write "How many cookies are left in the jar?" Children can write the answer on the back of the paper. In the sample below, seven cookies are left.

As an extra treat, provide mini-cookies or crackers for children to use as manipulatives—and to munch on—as they figure out their story.

# "Dragons and Giants"

### Before Reading

Ask children what they think it means to be brave. Have they ever been brave? Have they ever wished they had acted more bravely?

### During Reading

As you read, focus on the ideas of being brave and not brave. After each episode in which Frog and Toad escape danger, ask what they did that was brave.

### After Reading

Invite children to reflect on the story by asking:

❊ "Why is looking in the mirror a funny way to tell whether you are brave?"

❊ "Were Frog and Toad brave by the end? How did they act bravely? In what way didn't they act bravely?"

### Extending the Story

## Mood Mirrors

(Building Vocabulary, Drama)

Frog and Toad stood in front of the mirror and decided that they looked brave. Display a mirror and have children show what they think brave might look like.

Invite children to suggest other words or expressions that might describe the way they are looking, such as *courageous* or *fierce*.

Then give a hand mirror to pairs of children and multiple copies of page 34 to each child. Have children take turns using different facial expressions as they look in the mirror. Then encourage them to think of words that describe their expressions and write their favorites on the mirror patterns. Display the mood mirrors with the title "Mood Mirror Words." Have children walk past acting out each of the words on the mirrors as they go.

## Different Kinds of Bravery

(Social Studies, Writing)

Have children talk about what it means to brave. Encourage them to recognize the many dimensions of bravery, such as standing up for a friend or something that they believe in.

Have children tell their own bravery stories. They can do this by drawing and writing, by creating a dramatic scene and acting it out, or by creating clay figures of the scene. Talk about the kinds of bravery they have shared.

Reward students with bravery badges (see pattern, below). Encourage them to wear their badges home and share their bravery stories with family members. (Affix them to children's clothing with bubbles of tape on the back.)

**badge pattern**

# "The Dream"

## Before Reading

Invite children to share their thoughts about dreams. Ask:

✳ "How are dreams different from real life?"

✳ "What kinds of things might happen in a dream that wouldn't happen in real life?"

✳ "What kinds of things are the same as in real life?"

## During Reading

Focus on how Toad's dream is portrayed and the conflict Toad is having between his love of Frog and his desire to be "better" than Frog.

✳ "Which parts of the story seem like a dream?"

✳ "Why do you think Toad is having this dream? What is he feeling about Frog?"

✳ "Why do you think Frog is getting smaller? What does that show?"

## After Reading

Talk about the ending. What do children think Toad learned from the dream? Have they ever wanted to be better at something than a friend or sibling? What does the story ending tell them about Toad's real feelings about Frog?

## Extending the Story

### Dream Art (Art, Writing)

Point out that much of the world's great art has come from dreams. If possible, show children paintings in the surrealist style (for example, works by Dali, Rousseau, or Magritte). Then invite children to paint real or made-up dreams. Talk about some features of dreams that can be expressed visually. For example:

◎ In dreams, things can be bigger or smaller than in real life.

◎ In dreams, things can be different colors than in real life.

◎ In dreams, things can be together that wouldn't be in real life (for example, a tiger in a living room).

Have children draw or paint their real or made-up dreams. Share their work. Then invite children to make dreamcatchers, right, to help let in good dreams or keep out bad ones.

## Make a Dreamcatcher

(Art, Social Studies)

Explain that long ago, Native American tribes such as the Ojibwe (whose traditional lands are around the Great Lakes) used something called a dreamcatcher that they believed would keep bad dreams away. A small hole left in the center of the dreamcatcher allows good dreams to come in. Invite children to make their own dreamcatchers. Then have them use their dreamcatchers to let in or keep out the dreams they talk about in class.

**What You Need:**
✳ small paper plates
✳ scissors
✳ hole punch
✳ lengths of yarn, about 6 1/2 feet long
✳ beads and craft feathers (optional)

**1.** Cut out the center of the paper plate, leaving a wide rim. (For easier cutting, fold the plate in half and cut out a half circle starting from the folded side.)

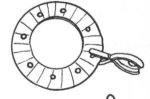

**2.** Punch eight evenly spaced holes around the rim.

**3.** Knot one end of the yarn through one of the holes. Tie a loop.

**4.** Weave the yarn through the holes, back and forth across the center of the ring, to create a web.

**5.** Leave about eight inches of yarn hanging free. Thread some beads through the yarn and tie on a few feathers, if desired.

# Mood Mirror

# Frog and Toad All Year

◆✳◆

## (HARPERCOLLINS, 1976)

The third book in the series, *Frog and Toad All Year* shows the two friends as they experience each of the four seasons. (The fifth story is reserved for Christmas.) Children will be delighted to read these seasonal stories about how Frog hunts for spring (which is "just around the corner"), how Toad tries to prevent ice cream from melting in the summer, and more.

## Book Talk

Following are some questions and discussion points for the individual stories:

**"Down the Hill"**

❋ "Why did Toad fall off the sled when he realized Frog wasn't there?"

❋ "Did Frog learn anything from the ride? What might another character have learned?"

**"The Corner"**

❋ "What is funny about this story?"

❋ "What doesn't the young frog realize about what his parents told him?"

❋ "How is Toad being a good friend?"

**"Ice Cream"**

❋ "Have you ever had an experience similar to Toad's when having ice cream?"

❋ "How do you think Frog would have acted if he had gone to get the ice cream instead of Toad?"

**"The Surprise"**

❋ "What is special about the surprise Frog and Toad plan for each other?"

❋ "Do you think it matters that the leaves blew back? Why or why not?"

**"Christmas Eve"**

❋ "What made Toad think was Frog was late?"

❋ "Why was the clock such a good gift for Toad?"

❋ "Have you ever worried about something only to find out later that everything was alright after all?"

## Extending the Stories

### Just Around the Corner (Building Vocabulary)

In the story "The Corner," Frog hears that spring is "just around the corner," so that is where he looks for it. Invite children to talk about what the expression means.

Ask children whether they have heard any of the following expressions. Together, discuss them. Try to use them in sentences.

- He is in hot water.
- Don't count your chickens before they hatch.
- Nip it in the bud.
- Have a change of heart.
- That makes my skin crawl.
- I put myself in her shoes.

Then pick one simple expression, such as *in hot water*. Have children think of a situation in which Toad or Frog might be in hot water. What funny things might they say or do around the idea of being in hot water?

Children may want to write a new story—or make a drawing with a caption—showing a humorous situation in which Frog or Toad takes an idiomatic expression too literally.

### Triple-Decker Comprehension Cones
(Identifying Main Idea and Details)

Encourage children to identify the main idea and supporting details in the story "Ice Cream." Provide construction paper in an assortment of ice cream colors, along with tan or brown for the cones. Tell children to cut out three round scoops of ice cream and one triangle-shaped cone each. Then direct them to write the title and main idea of the story on the cone and a detail that supports the main idea on each of the ice cream scoops. Have children tape the parts together. Display the cones on a bulletin board, and encourage children to talk about what they have written.

# Days With Frog and Toad

◆ ✳ ◆

## (HARPERCOLLINS, 1979)

**D**ays With Frog and Toad is the last book in the Frog and Toad series. In this volume, Frog and Toad fly kites, clean house, and tell ghost stories together. While the stories are every bit as funny and charming as those in the previous volumes, there is a bittersweet mood that makes Days With Frog and Toad a wonderful place to end your Frog and Toad studies.

## Book Talk

Ask children to pay particular attention to the last story, "Alone," which tells of a day Frog feels like being alone and how Toad adjusts to this idea. The last image of the book, in which Frog and Toad sit "alone together" on their own little island, sums up the richness of their friendship. Ask, "What does 'being alone together' mean? Why is this a good thing?" Other discussion points for the individual stories include:

### "Tomorrow"

❋ "What advice would you give Toad to stop him from worrying about tomorrow?"

❋ "What do you think Frog is feeling about Toad?"

❋ "How does Toad feel when the kite keeps crashing?"

### "The Kite"

❋ "Think of a time when you tried to learn something new. Have you ever felt like Toad does when his kite keeps crashing?"

❋ "Why do you think Frog tells Toad to keep trying to fly the kite when Toad wants to give up?"

### "Shivers"

❋ "Do you think having the shivers can be a good feeling? In what way?"

❋ "Why do you think Frog and Toad feel that way?"

### "The Hat"

❋ "Why do you think Toad tells Frog that he likes the hat just as it is?"

❋ "Why does Frog tell Toad to think big thoughts so that he will grow into the hat?"

❋ "Think about what Frog did with the hat. Was this a nice trick to play? Why or why not?"

## Extending the Stories

### Fly a Kite the Frog and Toad Way
(Reading and Following Directions, Art)

In "The Kite," Frog and Toad fly a kite. Invite children to make their own kites as they practice the important skill of reading and following directions. Give each child a copy of page 37 with the materials listed.

After making the kites, review with children the actions that Frog said helped to get the kite off the ground. Then start a new action word list. Invite children to write their own silly actions on the bows attached to their kites' tails.

### Alone-Together Poems (Poetry)

After reading the story "Alone," ask children whether they think wanting to be alone always means being unhappy, as Toad believes. Or are they like Frog, and can they think of times that they wanted to be alone because they were happy?

On chart paper, label one column "Alone" and a second column "Together." Ask children questions, such as "When do you want to be alone? What kinds of things do you do or think when you are having fun alone? What kinds of things are more fun doing together?" Write down their ideas. Then give each child a copy of page 38. Have children use the frame as a basis for writing poems on this theme. They can model their poem's structure on the sample below:

| I Like to Be Alone | I Like to Be Together |
|---|---|
| I like to be alone when I want to read a book. | I like to be together when I cook with my brother. |
| I like to be alone and play with my stuffed animals and make up all the rules. | I like to be together when I make mud pies with my friend. |
| I like to be alone when I am looking at the sky. | I like to be together when my mom reads to me. |

# How to Make a Kite

**What You Need:**

- ☆ 8-inch square of colored paper
- ☆ 12-inch piece of string or yarn
- ☆ colored paper scraps
- ☆ pencil
- ☆ scissors
- ☆ glue

**1** Fold a sheet of paper in half on the diagonal. It will make a triangle. Then unfold it.

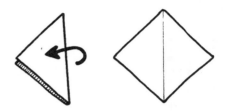

**2** Fold in the two sides so that they meet in the middle, forming two triangles.

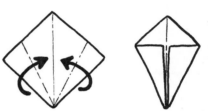

**3** Glue or tape a piece of yarn or string to your kite. Then turn it over.

**4** Cut out the bow pattern. Trace bows on scraps of colored paper. Then cut them out.

**5** Glue the bows to the string of your kite. Then decorate your kite!

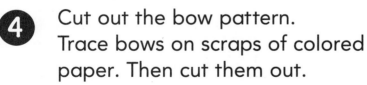

bow pattern

Name _____

Date _____

# Alone–Together Poetry Frame

I like to be alone

I like to be together
_____
_____.

I like to be alone

I like to be together
_____
_____.

I like to be alone

I like to be together
_____
_____.

Teaching With Favorite Arnold Lobel Books    Scholastic Teaching Resources

# Tying It All Together

Use these activities after reading any of the Frog and Toad Stories.

## Talk About the Books

Ask questions about each book as a whole.

❋ Discuss the characters of Frog and Toad. (Refer to your Frog and Toad Are Different chart, page 19, if you have made one.) Ask, "What do you think of Frog and Toad? Which one do you think is funnier? Which one do you like the best?"

❋ "How do you think Frog and Toad help each other? In which stories did Frog help Toad? In which stories did Toad help Frog?"

❋ "Which stories did you think were mostly funny? Which stories were mostly serious?"

❋ "In which stories did Frog and Toad enjoy being together? In which stories was being together a problem?"

❋ If you have been filling in the Who and What Starts It chart on page 28, take time to review it.

## Create Two Animal Friends

(Writing)

Have children use Frog and Toad as models for creating characters of their own. Since Frog and Toad have such different personalities, encourage children to consider making their two characters opposites in some way. Use this as an opportunity to discuss opposites. For example, ask:

❋ "If one character loves to talk, what might the other character be like?"

❋ "If one character loves sports, what might the other character be like?"

To extend the example of Frog and Toad, children may want to pick two animals that are close in type (for example, an ant and a beetle, or a lion and a tiger). Children can also use this as an opportunity to research the differences between these pairs of similar animals.

## Focus on Friendship

(Language Arts, Social Studies)

Talk about Frog and Toad's friendship. How do the different stories show different aspects of what it means to be a friend? You may want to review the stories by making a chart such as the one below. Also encourage children to share their own experiences with friendship.

### What It Means to Be a Friend

| Story | How Frog and Toad Act Like Friends |
|---|---|
| Spring | They greet the spring together and think of all the fun they will have. |
| The Story | Frog and Toad tell each other stories when they are sick. |
| The Kite | Frog encourages Toad to keep trying to fly the kite. |
| Christmas Eve | Toad worries about Frog because he is late. |

## Friendship Scrapbooks (Writing, Art)

Invite children to make a "Frog and Toad Are Friends" class scrapbook. Ask children to imagine that Frog and Toad are making a scrapbook of the events in the stories. Which events might they choose to include? What would they say about them in the captions? Give children large sheets of heavyweight paper. Invite them to draw or use craft materials to depict favorite story events, and write short captions for them from either Frog's or Toad's point of view. Then bind the pages together to make a class book.

# The World of Frog and Toad
## Diorama (Exploring Setting, Art)

The illustrations in Arnold Lobel's books offer many clues about what Frog and Toad's world looks like. Have children choose one or more of the books' settings to re-create in diorama form. If your class has been keeping an Arnold Lobel's World chart (see page 9), review it before starting. Have materials such as the following on hand for children to create with:

* twigs, leaves, stones, and other natural objects
* clay (to create caves and other natural formations)
* crepe paper and pipe cleaners (for the flowers in Toad's garden)
* small milk cartons (for Frog and Toad's homes)
* aluminum foil or small mirrors (for the pond in *Frog and Toad All Year*)

## Frog and Toad's Paint Palette (Art)

No matter what season it is, Arnold Lobel's world always has a soft and gentle feeling. Part of this is due to his distinctive palette. Most of Lobel's stories are illustrated using a three-color printing process rather than the usual four-color. The subtle tones are also achieved by mixing the colors with black to "gray" them.

Invite children to create paintings of Frog and Toad's world using this type of palette. Set out blue, brown, yellow, and black paint, and leave plenty of room for mixing. Remind children that they can make different shades of green by blending blue and yellow. Have children paint pictures of Frog and Toad's forest, home, and other parts of their world.

---

## Author's Craft

# Endings Grab Bag
### (Analyzing Story Endings)

Arnold Lobel wrote his endings very carefully. Not only do they provide closure to the stories but they often reflect on the stories' more subtle dimensions. Have children focus on the last lines by playing Endings Grab Bag.

1. Display a bag labeled "Endings." Invite children to choose a favorite story.

2. Have them look up the last lines and write them on sheets of paper. (Last lines can be loosely defined as one to three sentences.)

3. Put the pages in the grab bag and ask volunteers to pick a last line from the bag and read it to the class.

4. Have the class try to figure out which story it came from. Ask how they could tell the last line came from that story. What does the ending say about the story? Finally, ask, "Do you think it's a good last line? Why or why not?"

> They stayed there for a long time, just feeling brave together.
>
> **(from "Dragons and Giants," in *Frog and Toad Together*)**

> They were having the shivers. It was a good, warm feeling.

**(from "Shivers," in *Days With Frog and Toad*)**

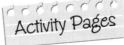

## Activity Pages

### Exploring Character

Use the activities on pages 41–42 to help children further explore the characters of Frog and Toad. These activities are useful for helping children distinguish between the thoughts, feelings, and points of view of Frog and Toad—two very different characters.

# Pick a Point of View

Choose a story or part of a story and tell it first from Frog's point of view.
Then tell the same story from Toad's point of view.

| **Frog Tells It** | **Toad Tells It** |
|---|---|
| It started when | It started when |
| _____ | _____ |
| _____. | _____. |
| Next, | Next, |
| _____ | _____ |
| _____. | _____. |
| Finally, | Finally, |
| _____ | _____ |
| _____. | _____. |
| I liked it when | I liked it when |
| _____ | _____ |
| _____. | _____. |
| I didn't like it when | I didn't like it when |
| _____ | _____ |
| _____. | _____. |

Name _____ Date _____

# My Best Friend

What does Frog think of Toad? What does Toad think of Frog? Imagine that you are Frog or Toad. Use information from the stories to fill in these sentences:

| **Frog Is My Best Friend** | **Toad Is My Best Friend** |
|---|---|
| I liked it when Frog _____ _____ . | I liked it when Toad _____ _____ . |
| I didn't like it when Frog _____ _____ . | I didn't like it when Toad _____ _____ . |
| Frog and I had fun when _____ _____ . | Toad and I had fun when _____ _____ . |
| Frog is a great friend because _____ _____ . | Toad is a great friend because _____ _____ . |

# Grasshopper on the Road

❖ ❈ ❖

## (HARPERCOLLINS, 1978)

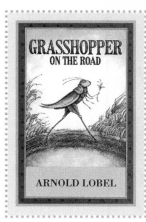

Grasshopper on the Road follows the classic novel form called picaresque in which a character travels and has a series of adventures. In this engaging and clever tale, Grasshopper sets off on a journey and encounters a variety of other animal characters that embody different kinds of personalities and approaches to life. Grasshopper has a chance to compare his take on life to theirs. Through their encounter with this wonderful book, children can explore different approaches to daily life and the problems and opportunities it affords.

## Threading Through the Book

### Who Does What? Chart (Comparing and Contrasting Characters)

To fully understand characters, it is important to see them in relation to other characters. Conflict—having different opinions or different ways of viewing a situation—is an important part of character development. *Grasshopper on the Road* lets children see this in action, as Grasshopper sometimes takes an attitude similar to that of many of the characters he meets and at other times takes one that differs from theirs.

Start a Who Does What? chart. After reading each story, have children describe the central situation. Then have them note the responses of Grasshopper and the other characters. Have them analyze whether their attitudes are more similar or more different.

### Who Does What?

| Story | Situation | Grasshopper | Other Characters | Similar or Different |
|-------|-----------|-------------|------------------|---------------------|
| **The Club** | Grasshopper meets beetles celebrating the morning. | likes all times of day | The beetles only like the morning. | different |
| **A New House** | Grasshopper accidentally causes the worm to lose his home in the apple. | feels bad about the worm and is happy when the worm can find a new home | The worm reasons that losing his apple is a good thing and looks forward to his new home. | similar |

### Using the Introduction

The introduction on page 6 sets up the journey. Talk about the phrase "getting there is half the fun." Tell children that in this book, for Grasshopper "getting there is the whole fun." Talk about trips they've taken. Did they look forward to the journey? Were there things they were worried about?

Then talk about Grasshopper's statement, "This road looks fine to me." Ask, "What does this show about how Grasshopper feels about life?" Make a list of words that describe his attitude, such as *carefree, happy, adventurous, free,* and *bold.*

## Connecting to Other Arnold Lobel Books

❖ ❈ ❖

If children have read *Owl at Home* or the Frog and Toad stories, they will find that Grasshopper is a more stable and adult character than any they have met so far. However, many of the characters he encounters in his journeys are similar to the childlike and lovably anxious Owl or Toad.

As a more grown-up character, Grasshopper can serve as a role model for children who are learning to take a more independent stance in life. Other characters, such as Uncle Elephant, can also act as role models. While Uncle Elephant is a parent figure, Grasshopper is like an older sibling whom children can try to imitate with his self-assured, happy, and confident view of life.

# "The Club"

## Before Reading

Ask children if they have ever seen a group carrying signs to express an opinion. Talk about what it means to try to influence someone to agree with you.

## During Reading

Pause after the beetles give Grasshopper a sign saying "MORNING IS TOPS." Ask, "Why are they so happy with Grasshopper? Why do they want to let him into their club?" Then stop again after a beetle has called Grasshopper stupid for liking afternoon and evening, too. Ask, "What has changed?"

## After Reading

Help children safely discuss issues such as narrow thinking and being left out of a group by focusing on the beetles and Grasshopper. Ask,

❋ "What do you think of the beetles' change in attitude toward Grasshopper?"

❋ "What do you like or not like about how Grasshopper reacts to them?"

❋ "How might you act if you were Grasshopper?"

## Extending the Story

### "Many Ways to Be" Posters
(Social Studies)

Help children understand group dynamics with this activity. Give each child three large unlined index cards. Ask children to write their favorite color on the first card, their favorite season on the second card, and on the third card, the title of their favorite book. Have children tape each card to a craft stick to make a small sign.

Call out "colors," and holding up their color signs, have children move into groups according to their favorite color. Give children time to look around and share the reason for their color choice. Then call out "season," and have children regroup according to their favorite season. Finally, do the same for favorite book.

Call the class back together for a discussion and record notes on the chalkboard to summarize the main ideas. Ask children what they noticed being in the different groups. Elicit thoughts about how children viewed other groups and how the groups changed according to the different criteria.

## Author's Craft

### Dew Rhymes With New (Exploring Rhyme)

On pages 12–13 of this story, one of the beetles asks, "When does the clover sparkle with dew?" and "When is the sunshine yellow and new?" Ask children what they notice about these two lines. (*The last word in each sentence rhymes; the two words have the same spelling pattern.*) Talk about how the author's use of rhyme helps to emphasize the celebratory mood of the beetles. Then try this activity to help children learn other words that include the variant vowel word family *-ew*.

1. Write the following initial consonants, consonant clusters, and consonant digraphs on large index cards. Write these letters near the right edge of each card: *d, f, n, p, bl, ch, cr, dr, fl, gr, kn, sl, st, scr, thr*. Then write the word family *-ew* on another large index card.

2. Tape each card to a craft stick to make a miniature letter sign.

3. Ask a volunteer to hold up the *-ew* sign. Then randomly pass out the initial consonant cards to different students.

4. Tell children to pretend they are the beetles in the story and invite them to march around the classroom holding their signs up high, just as the beetles did. Then ask, "How can we make the word *new*?" The child holding the *n* card should march over to the child holding the *-ew* sign. Invite everyone to say the word together and then call out, "N-E-W spells *new*!"

Continue challenging children to form new words by substituting letters.

**Tip:** Recycle! Write the rhyming words on the reverse sides of the signs children made for the activity above.

# "A New House"

## Before Reading

Brainstorm with children a list of animals and their homes. Then tell children that they are going to read a story in which the fact that a worm lives in an apple is very important.

## During Reading

Ask, "How did Grasshopper feel when he took a bite out of the apple and found out it was the worm's home? How would you have felt?"

## After Reading

This is an opportunity to explore a character who is more similar to Grasshopper in his attitude toward life than some of the other characters. Ask children to briefly describe what the worm is like (*takes things in stride, looks on the bright side of things*). Ask, "How is this similar to Grasshopper?" Have children find passages in the story that illustrate their character descriptions of the worm and of Grasshopper. Suggest that they summarize this for the Who Does What? chart (page 43).

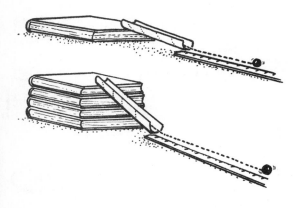

## Extending the Story

### What's Inside an Apple? (Science)

In the story, the worm used an apple for a house, complete with an attic, a cellar, and all the rooms in between. What's really inside an apple? Help children sharpen their observation skills to find out. Divide the class into small groups and give each an apple cut in half crosswise. Ask children to draw what they observe. Prompt them to notice details by asking questions, such as "What does the core look like? Where are the seeds? How many are there?" (*The star-shaped core is composed of five chambers. Each chamber usually holds two seeds.*) Follow up by asking each group to show their drawings and share their findings. How many seeds did each group's apple have?

### Roll, Apple, Roll! (Science)

Reread the section of the story about the apple rolling down the hill. Ask, "What do you think made the apple roll?" Children may mention the apple's roundness and the hill. Then say, "The apple rolled to the bottom of the hill, hit a tree, and smashed into pieces. If the tree hadn't been there, how far do you think the apple might have rolled?" Tell children that they are going to investigate to find out.

**1.** Gather ten books, each about 1/2-inch thick, a marble, and a yardstick or meter stick. Make a ramp by cutting a paper towel tube in half lengthwise, as shown. Find a place with a smooth floor. Lean the ramp against one book.

**2.** Give each child a copy of How Far Will It Roll? (page 50). Then tell children that the marble is the apple and the ramp (the half tube) is the hill. Hold the marble at the top of the ramp. Then let it go. Measure from the bottom of the ramp how far the marble rolls. Have children record the results.

**3.** Ask them to predict: "What will happen if we make a steeper hill?" Raise the ramp to four books, then seven books, then ten books. Have children record their predictions and then repeat step 2 each time. Which height made the marble roll farthest? (*The marble usually rolls farthest at seven books. With ten books, the distance drops off. Why? The sharp incline of ten books causes the marble to hit the bottom of the ramp sharply before it begins to roll. This impact slows it down.*)

# "The Sweeper"

## Before Reading

Talk with children about cleaning chores such as dusting and sweeping. Ask, "What things need to be cleaned up in our classroom? Who does these chores? How often do you think they need to be done?" Then tell children that they are going to read a story about a housefly that gets carried away with cleaning.

## During Reading

After reading about how the housefly first swept its rug, then its floor, and then the whole house, stop and ask children what they think the housefly might do next.

## After Reading

Have children discuss their impressions of the housefly. Ask, "Why do you think the housefly wants to clean everything up—even things that don't need cleaning? What words would you use to describe him?" Talk about why the housefly is happy with what he is doing.

## Author's Craft

### Yes, Yes, Yes,
#### (Using Repetitive Language)

Point out that in this story, Arnold Lobel uses repetitive language to get a feeling across. The language matches the action in the story, because the housefly's actions are very repetitive.

Have children find the places in the story that have repetitive words. (*"clean, clean, clean"; "sweep, sweep, sweep"; "no, no, no"*) Then have children try their hand at writing a paragraph that uses this technique. First, have them think of a situation where the action might be repetitive. Then have them describe that action.

## Extending the Story

### Sweep the S-Blends! (Phonics)

This story includes several examples of words that begin with *s*-blends (*speck, stones, sticks, sweep*). On chart paper, write these blends. Then challenge children to find in the story examples of words that begin with these blends. Brainstorm other words that begin with these blends. Then play a game to extend learning.

1. Using light brown construction paper, make 15 circles, each about six inches wide. These are the stones for the path.

2. Use a marker to write each of the following blends on five stones: *sp, st, sw*. Randomly place the stones in a winding path on the floor, securing them with tape.

3. To play, divide the class into two teams. Give each team a toy broom. Players take turns rolling a number cube, moving the number of spaces indicated, gently sweeping each stone in their path.

4. To stay on a stone, players must say a word that begins with the blend on that stone, or return to the previous position. The first team to reach the end of the walk wins.

# "The Voyage"

## Before Reading

❋ Ask children, "Can you think of a situation where someone offered you help?"

❋ Then ask, "What if someone offered you help and you didn't need it?" Tell children that they are going to read a story in which that is exactly what happens to Grasshopper.

## During Reading

Pause after reading, " 'Well then,' said Grasshopper, 'there is only one thing for me to do.' " Ask children to predict what they think might happen next.

## After Reading

❋ Elicit that Grasshopper carried the mosquito across the puddle and not vice versa by asking, "Who carried whom across the puddle?"

❋ Then ask, "Why did Grasshopper want to make the mosquito feel that he was the one helping?" Have children discuss whether or not they think this was the best way to act.

## Extending the Story

### Helping Hand (Writing)

Have children think about something they can do on their own, such as crossing the street at a green light or crosswalk while looking both ways. Tell children to imagine themselves in a situation in which someone offered to help them do this—but that they didn't really want or need the help—just like Grasshopper in the story.

Have them craft a short piece of realistic fiction (one or two paragraphs) that includes what they would tell the person who offered to help. Explain that we call this kind of writing realistic fiction because, although it is based on real-life events and could happen, it is not exactly what did happen.

### Float a Boat (Science)

Ask children to predict what would have happened if Grasshopper had gotten into the boat. (*It probably would have sunk*.) But how much weight could the boat have held? Invite children to find out.

Divide the class into small groups and give each group a dishpan of water, pieces of aluminum foil, and a supply of pennies. Tell children to make a boat out of a piece of foil and then set it on the water. Have children predict how many pennies they can put in the boat before it sinks, then test to find out.

Afterward, have the class share results. Ask children to think about why results may vary. For a fun follow-up, share the delightful story, *Who Sank the Boat?* by Pamela Allen (Putnam and Grosset, 1982).

# "Always"

Talk with children about their daily routines. Ask them to name things they do every day that they might not notice (*for example, eat lunch with the same friends, sit in the same seat at school*). What things do they do differently every day? Tell children they are going to read a story in which some butterflies do the same things each day.

Point out the italicized words as you read (*always* on page 44, *this* on page 50, and *different* on page 52). Then reread the sentences in which each word appears, first without emphasis on the italicized words and then with extra emphasis. Ask children to describe the difference between the two versions. How does the meaning change?

Ask, "What would it feel like to be the butterflies and have the exact same routine every day? What would it feel like to be Grasshopper and do something new every day?" Guide children to understand that there are advantages and disadvantages to both.

## Compound Word Search (Word Analysis)

*Grasshopper* and *butterflies* are just two of the compound words in this story. Have children find these words on the first page. What do they notice about them? Then challenge children to search the story—and even the rest of the book—for other examples of compound words. Examples include *mushroom, afternoon, sunflower, housefly, dragonflies,* and *sunset.*

Record the words on a sheet of chart paper. Invite volunteers to draw a line between the two words that make up each compound word. Ask children to explain how each pair of words works together to form the meaning of the compound word.

Then give children practice working with compound words: On separate index cards, write each part of a compound word. Mix up the cards and give one to each child. Ask children to roam the room until they find a classmate whose word card forms a compound word with theirs.

## Butterfly Symmetry Chains
(Math, Science, Art)

Reinforce the idea of the butterflies' repeating routine and explore the symmetry of their wings with this activity.

1. Cut sheets of 11- by 17-inch paper in half the long way. Give each child a strip.

2. Direct children to make accordion folds, two inches deep, along one of the short ends of the paper. (They will make seven folds.)

3. Have children draw half of a butterfly's wings on the folded paper.

4. Model how to cut out the butterfly pattern making sure not to cut completely through the folds on each side. Next, invite children to cut out small shapes from the folded pattern, then unfold the paper.

Guide children to notice that the designs on each side of each butterfly are the same. Explain that something is symmetrical when it is exactly the same on both sides of a dividing line.

# "At Evening"

## Before Reading

Ask children to imagine they are going down a country road in a car. What do they think they might see from the car? Then ask, "Suppose you were walking down that same road. What might you see?" Tell children they are going to read a story in which some animals go fast while Grasshopper goes slowly down a road.

## During Reading

Ask children who they would rather be, Grasshopper, walking slowly, or the dragonflies, flying fast. Why?

## After Reading

Have children discuss what the dragonflies see as they are zooming about and what Grasshopper sees as he walks slowly down the road. Ask, "What do the dragonflies miss by going so fast?"

### Author's Craft

## Zipping and Zooming
### (Using Descriptive Words)

Have children search the story for vivid verbs that describe movement. Explain that a vivid verb is one that describes the action in a lively way that makes a clear picture in your mind of what is happening. Examples in the story include *zipping*, *zooming*, *looping*, *spinning*, *diving*, and *dipping*.

Then have children brainstorm a list of vivid verbs to describe walking, running, and jumping. Suggest that they choose five words from the list and write a short poem using them.

## Extending the Story

### Poetic Pictures (Language Arts, Art)

"The sun was going down. The world was soft and quiet." This passage, at the beginning of the story, is paired with a picture of a muted red sun at dusk. It is one of several evocative passages that describe the changes that occur as day turns to night. Invite children to look for other examples in the text and illustrations.

Then give children scrap paper and watercolor paints and brushes, colored pencils, or pastels. How might they use the art supplies to show shadows, a sunset, or darkness setting in? Give children time to experiment, and then give them sheets of art paper. Invite them to choose a description from the story to depict and use the art materials to capture the look and feel of the setting.

### Take a Close-Up Look
(Science, Art, Writing)

Invite children to make binoculars they can use outdoors that will help them focus on details in the world around them. For each pair, you'll need two empty bathroom tissue tubes, masking tape, and a two-foot length of string.

Show children how to place the tubes side by side and tape them together using masking tape. Have them punch a hole on the outside edge of each tube, then knot one end of the string through each hole.

Invite children to personalize their binoculars, using markers, stickers, and other art materials. Then take children outdoors to use their binoculars and write about the things they observe through them.

Name _____

Date _____

# How Far Will It Roll?

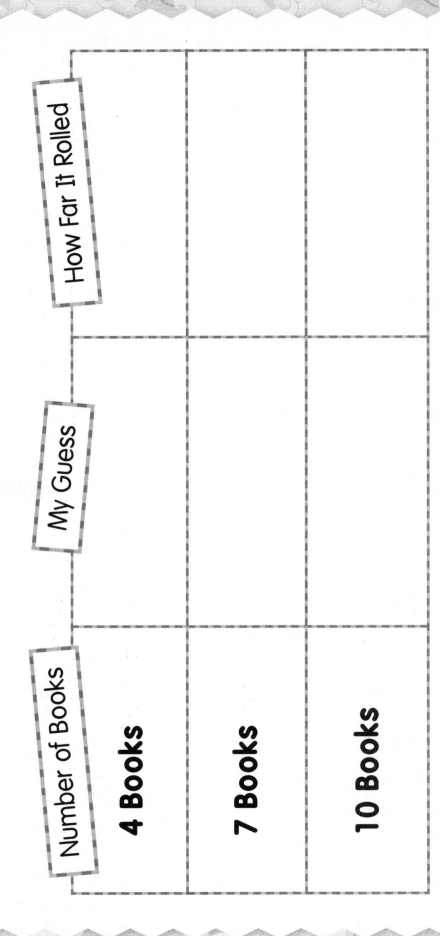

| Number of Books | My Guess | How Far It Rolled |
|---|---|---|
| **4 Books** | | |
| **7 Books** | | |
| **10 Books** | | |

Teaching With Favorite Arnold Lobel Books    Scholastic Teaching Resources

# Tying It All Together

## Portrait of Grasshopper
(Identifying Character Traits)

Have a volunteer read aloud the final sentence of *Grasshopper on the Road*: "He knew that in the morning the road would still be there, taking him on and on to wherever he wanted to go." Use this as a jumping-off point to discuss Grasshopper's character. Ask, "What does this tell you about Grasshopper?"

Have children complete and review their Who Does What? chart (page 43). Talk about any insights they have gained into Grasshopper's character from studying the chart. Then encourage children to write a brief character sketch describing Grasshopper.

## The Further Adventures of Grasshopper (Writing)

Use the last sentence of the book to lead into another writing extension. What new adventures might Grasshopper have the following day? Tell children that they will write a story to add to Grasshopper's adventures on the road. Prompt them with the following suggestions:

 "First think of a character or group of characters Grasshopper might meet. Choose an insect or another tiny animal, such as those in the book."

 "Now think about what your characters will be like. What will they be doing when Grasshopper meets them?"

 "Decide whether Grasshopper is the same as or different from your new characters."

 "Now think of what the characters would say to each other when they meet."

 "Write and illustrate a story describing how they meet and what they say to each other."

Extend the activity by inviting children to team up and act out each other's stories for the rest of the class.

## How Do Creepy Crawlies Get Around?
(Science)

*Grasshopper on the Road* features a variety of insects and other creepy crawlies. One way to classify these creatures is by their main means of locomotion. Long, strong, jointed hind legs help a "hopper" such as a grasshopper leap into the air. "Flyers" such as butterflies rely on strong muscles in their wings to provide the power for flapping. In the case of "crawlers," such as worms or beetles, pairs of short legs or bristles propel these creatures along the ground.

Challenge children to classify the creatures in the story according to the way they move. Divide the class into groups. Give each group a copy of page 52. Have children cut apart the cards (besides the creepy crawlies named in the story, a few others have been added) and cut out the labels. Also give each group three one-yard lengths of yarn to form Venn diagram circles. Tell them to place one label inside each circle.

Then instruct children to place each creepy crawly in the circle where it best belongs. Do any of the creatures belong in more than one circle? How might children create overlapping areas to accommodate creatures that move in more than one way?

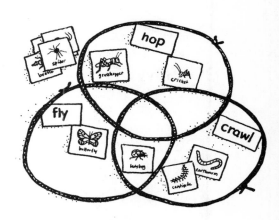

**Answers:** hop—grasshopper, cricket, and katydid; fly—dragonfly, butterfly, mosquito, and housefly; crawl—earthworm, centipede, spider, ladybug, and beetle. Examples that move in more than one way: some spiders hop; certain beetles, crickets, and katydids fly; and almost all the creatures (except dragonflies) can crawl.

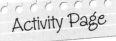
Activity Page

### Exploring Character and Setting

Use the Story Road Map on page 53 to help children recap the characters and settings in the story. You can use children's completed pages to assess their comprehension.

How Do Creepy Crawlies Get Around?

| **hop** | **fly** | **crawl** |
|---|---|---|
|  grasshopper |  ladybug |  beetle |
| 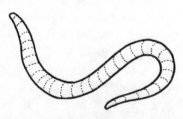 earthworm |  housefly |  mosquito |
|  butterfly |  dragonfly |  katydid |
|  centipede |  spider |  cricket |

*Teaching With Favorite Arnold Lobel Books*    Scholastic Teaching Resource

# Story Road Map

Here is a map of Grasshopper's travels. It shows his stops along the way. Tell about each place and who he meets. Use pictures and words.

Date _____

6

5

4

3

2

1

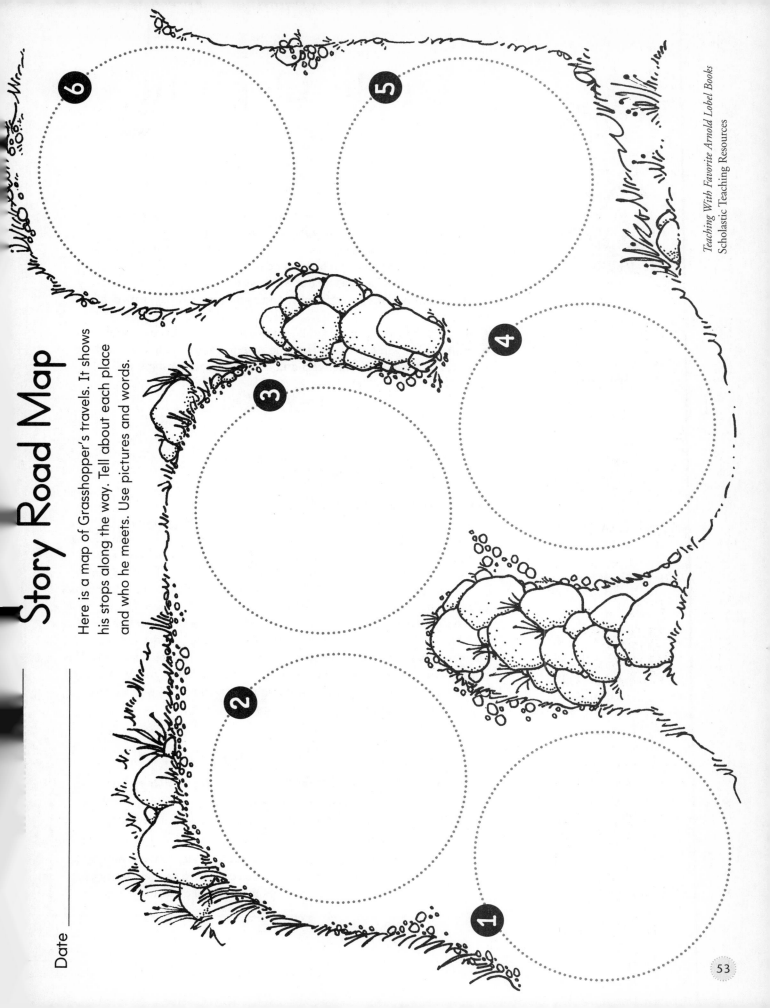

*Teaching With Favorite Arnold Lobel Books*
Scholastic Teaching Resources

# Uncle Elephant

◆ ✳ ◆

## (HarperCollins, 1981)

**U**ncle Elephant is one of Lobel's most heartwarming and touching stories. When the little elephant's parents seem to be missing at sea, Uncle Elephant arrives to save the day. He takes his nephew to visit him and entertains him with fanciful adventures and games. Happily, the parents return, but Uncle Elephant will miss the little elephant's company, for they have become great friends, and so they promise to visit each other often.

Reading this story can help children to overcome doubts and fears about the wide world they are learning to explore, and help them feel more confident in new endeavors and in forming relationships with significant adults in their lives.

### Connecting to Other Arnold Lobel Books

◆ ✳ ◆

**U**ncle Elephant is an important addition to the repertoire of any reader who has fallen in love with *Owl at Home*, the Frog and Toad books, or other Lobel titles. However, *Uncle Elephant* strikes a more serious chord than these other books. It touches on issues of loss and sadness and potentially offers children insight into how to deal with these feelings. Uncle Elephant represents the adult that children can turn to at these times. In addition, the way that Uncle Elephant faces his own aging and helps little elephant through adversity can be powerful tools for children in their own lives. This book can provide a safe and comfortable vehicle to gently discuss some of these concerns with children.

### Threading Through the Book

## What and Why Chart (Exploring Plot)

Because *Uncle Elephant* has a strong narrative structure, it is an ideal book to help children learn about plot. Although it is made up of a series of playful incidents, a format characteristic of most of Arnold Lobel's books, it is different because all these moments add up to a whole. This story has a definite beginning, middle, and end.

Whether he is piling on all his clothes at one time or showing his nephew the flowers in his garden, there is a reason for what Uncle Elephant does. Children may have the idea that the plot of a story involves simply *what* happens *when*. By keeping an ongoing What and Why chart, children can gain a more sophisticated understanding that why something happens is just as important as what happens.

### What and Why

| What Uncle Elephant Does | Why He Does This |
|---|---|
| He takes little elephant to visit him. | His parents have not come home. |
| He counts poles on the train. | so the little elephant will not get bored and sad on the journey and the time will go fast |

# CHAPTER 1: "Uncle Elephant Opens the Door"

## Before Reading

This chapter sets the stage for reading the whole book. Begin by asking children if they have an older relative they have ever visited. What did they learn from this person? What activities did they do together? Explain that they are going to read a story in which a little elephant visits his uncle for a very important reason.

## During Reading

✳ Encourage children to notice the problem that starts off this book. Ask them to think about what might happen in the rest of the story.

✳ Ask, "What do you think it will be like to visit Uncle Elephant?"

✳ Children may want to talk about how the little elephant feels as he sits in his lonely room and to share experiences of their own.

## After Reading

✳ Ask, "Why do you think Uncle Elephant talks to the little elephant about his wrinkles?"

✳ Uncle Elephant's fanciful description of his wrinkles is also a good jumping-off point to discuss attitudes about aging.

✳ Reread the passage in which Uncle Elephant says he has "more wrinkles than a tree has leaves." Talk about the metaphors he uses to describe his wrinkles. Invite children to think of other metaphors for Uncle Elephant's wrinkles.

## Extending the Story

### Make a Story Train
(Summarizing and Sequencing)

Tell children that by making a "story train," they will understand how this story moves along. Make multiple copies of page 64. (Enlarge, if desired.) To start, have children cut out the first car (the engine). Have them fill it in with the book's title and a brief summary of the problem in the first chapter. Children will add summaries of subsequent chapters in the other cars as they continue to read. (Make extra copies of the middle cars.) Have children glue their train cars, in order, onto large sheets of construction paper.

## Author's Craft

## Who's Talking?
(Exploring Point of View)

Explore point of view with children by guiding them to notice that *Uncle Elephant* is written in the first-person voice, and have children identify the character and who is speaking. Ask a volunteer to relate what happened to him or her on the way to school and write this down in a few sentences. Underline the words that indicate first-person point of view (*I, me, my,* and so on). Then have another child relate this same story as it happened, using the third-person voice (*he* or *she, his* or *her*). Talk about the shift in voice.

# CHAPTER 2: "Uncle Elephant Counts the Poles"

## Before Reading

Ask children to share experiences they may have had while traveling on a train. Ask, "What did you see out the window? How did you pass the time?" If children have not been on a train, encourage them to imagine what a train trip might be like.

## During Reading

Encourage children to notice what else Uncle Elephant counts besides telephone poles. (*horses, fields*) Discuss why he can't count these things very easily. Why are the peanuts easier to count?

## After Reading

Ask, "Why did Uncle Elephant count the poles?" Invite children to talk about activities and games they might have played while traveling.

## Extending the Story

### Pole Perspectives (Science)

Point out where Uncle Elephant says that the poles are moving by too fast to count. Ask children if they have ever looked outside while riding in a fast-moving vehicle (such as a train or car) and thought that the things outside the window were moving.

Explain that this is an optical illusion—a trick our brain plays on our eyes. Stationary objects such as telephone poles appear to be in motion because their position in our line of sight changes so rapidly. Our eyes continue to see the object for a fraction of a second after it has disappeared, creating the illusion of movement.

This phenomenon is also at work when we watch an animated cartoon. Make cartoon flip books to show how this works.

**1.** On the first page of a pad of sticky notes, draw a stick figure or other simple object near the outer edge of the page.

**2.** On the next page, draw the same object but move it in a little. Continue this process on each page of the pad.

**3.** To view, hold the pad by its bound edge, then quickly flip through the pages. What happens to the figure? Encourage children to record their observations in science journals.

### Story Fact Peanuts
(Identifying Story Elements)

Invite children to collect the elements of this story in a bag of peanuts! Enlarge and make multiple copies of the peanut pattern (left) for each child. Also give each child a small paper bag. On the outside of the bag, have children write the title of the story and their names.

Together, discuss the parts that make up a story (characters, setting, problem, solutions). Then encourage children to write on separate peanuts about each of these elements as they pertain to this story.

Have children put their peanuts in their bags and swap them with a classmate. Invite children to read and comment on each other's peanut story facts.

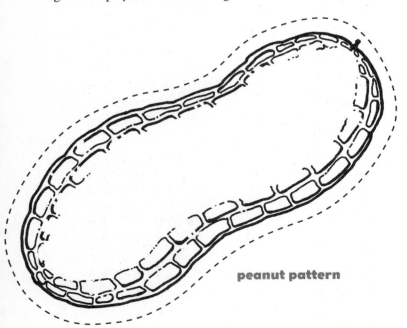

**peanut pattern**

# CHAPTER 3: "Uncle Elephant Lights a Lamp"

## Before Reading

Talk with children about wishes. Ask them to think of different stories they have read in which a character makes wishes. Then tell children that this chapter is about making wishes.

## During Reading

Pause after reading the part in which Uncle Elephant and the little elephant hear a small voice coming from inside the lamp. Ask children to say who they think is talking.

## After Reading

✳ Discuss the spider's wish. Ask, "How did the spider's wish differ from the elephants' wishes?"

✳ "What does Uncle Elephant do when he hears the spider's wish?" You might want to use this as an opportunity to talk about helping others when they ask for help.

✳ Talk about some of the reasons Uncle Elephant is making wishes and having the little elephant make wishes. Have children fill in their ideas on the What and Why chart (page 54). Also have them add to the Story Train (see pages 55 and 64).

## Extending the Story

### Magic Lamp Wish Book (Writing, Art)

What kinds of wishes would children make if they had a magic lamp? Let children write them down in their own magic lamp book.

Give each child multiple copies of the lamp pattern on page 65. Tell children to complete the sentence on each lamp by writing a special wish they have for themselves, their friends or family, or the world. Encourage them to write the reason for each wish as well. Them have them add a lamp-shaped cover and a title, and staple the pages to bind. Invite children to share their books and bring them home to read to family members.

## Author's Craft

# Polka-Dots and Stripes
## (Using Descriptive Words)

One of Uncle Elephant's wishes is for a polka-dot suit with striped pants. What other patterns or designs might he wish for? Talk with children about words that describe different patterns or designs on clothing (for example, *swirls*, *lines*, *loops*, *curls*).

Hand out paper and crayons or markers. Invite children to draw pictures of Uncle Elephant's clothing and cut them out. (Or copy the jacket pattern on page 66, first masking out the text.) Then have them draw a distinct pattern or design on each article of clothing and create a separate word label that describes it. Make a bulletin board display titled "Uncle Elephant's Fantastic Fashions" to showcase children's creations.

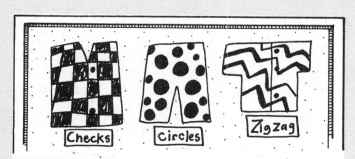

# CHAPTER 4: "Uncle Elephant Trumpets the Dawn"

## Before Reading

Ask children, "What time do you wake up in the morning? Is it light outside? How do you feel when you see the sunlight?" Tell children they will read about how Uncle Elephant greets the day.

## During Reading

※ After reading the first word of the story, ask, "Why do you think this word is in capital letters?" Then ask them what might be making the loud noise.

※ Pause again on page 27, and ask, "What do you think Uncle Elephant means when he says, 'Every new day deserves a good loud trumpet'?"

※ Then ask, "How could trumpeting the dawn help you during the day?" As you continue reading, invite children to join in whenever Uncle Elephant trumpets "VOOMAROOOM!"

## After Reading

※ Discuss Uncle Elephant's positive attitude toward the day. Talk about ways children might express happiness at the day when they wake up.

※ Talk about the meaning of the idea of being a "prince" or a "king" in a place, the way that Uncle Elephant and the little elephant are in the garden. Ask children if they have ever felt that way in a place that was special to them.

 Books About Flowers

*The Flower Alphabet Book* by Jerry Pallotta (Charlesbridge, 1990)

*National Audubon Society First Field Guide: Wildflowers* (Scholastic, 1998)

## Extending the Story

### Flower Crowns (Art)

Uncle Elephant and the little elephant make crowns, using the flowers in the garden. Let children design and create their own royal flower crowns to wear!

Wrap a sentence strip around each child's head and staple to fit. Then invite children to create different kinds of flowers using crepe paper, tissue paper, construction paper, pipe cleaners, glue, and other art materials. Children can tape, glue, or staple the flowers around their crown. Invite children to wear their crowns as they reread this chapter to one another.

### Flower Field Guide Collaborative Book
(Science, Writing, Art)

Begin by having children help you list the varieties of flowers named in this chapter. (*roses, daisies, daffodils, marigolds*) Then help children look in gardening books and field guides to locate these flowers and read about them.

Next, invite the class to make a collaborative field guide to flowers. Bring in gardening and seed catalogs that include pictures and descriptions of different kinds of flowers. Have children cut out the pictures, paste them on separate sheets of paper, and then research and write a few flower facts that tell about their choices (for example, what the flowers grow from—seeds, bulbs; where they grow; what colors they might be).

# CHAPTER 5: "Uncle Elephant Feels the Creaks"

## Before Reading

Read children the title of this chapter and then ask, "What do you think 'the creaks' are?"

## During Reading

After reading the first two pages of the chapter, ask children to describe what Uncle Elephant means when he says, "I am feeling the creaks." Then ask, "Why does Uncle Elephant feel so many creaks? What makes him feel better?"

## After Reading

Ask, "Why do you think it would make Uncle Elephant feel better to tell a story?" (*because he likes doing things for others, and this makes him forget about himself*)

## Author's Craft

# So Many Creaks
(Using Repetitive Language)

Point out that the way Arnold Lobel has Uncle Elephant repeat the word *creaks* makes the reader almost feel the creaks in his back. Explain that writers often use repeating words to achieve a special effect.

Have children brainstorm a list of words that could be repeated to achieve an effect. Tell them to choose interesting words that bear repeating. They might choose a sound, an exclamation, a vivid verb, or a quirky adjective. Then have children each choose a word from the list (they may overlap in their choices) and write a paragraph or poem that repeats this word.

## Extending the Story

### Readers' Theater With Uncle Elephant (Building Fluency)

Use the dialogue in this chapter to help children build fluency skills such as intonation and phrasing.

◎ To model how to make the voices of each character distinct, read aloud part of the chapter, using somewhat exaggerated expression. Then, on a rereading, ask children to read aloud with you.

◎ Also help children learn to pay attention to punctuation such as exclamation points. Read the sentence, "'Ouch!' cried Uncle Elephant," first with and then without the emphasis provided by the exclamation point. Each time, invite children to echo your reading. Then ask them to describe how the two readings change the meaning.

Then pair up students. Designate one child to read the part of Uncle Elephant. The other child will play the little elephant. Give children time to practice, paying attention to the good reading behaviors they reviewed with you.

When partners feel confident with their readings, invite them to read and act out the chapter for their classmates. If possible, provide a comfy chair and footstool for Uncle Elephant to use as he reads his lines!

# CHAPTER 6: "Uncle Elephant Tells a Story"

## Before Reading

After reading the title of this chapter, ask children to think about how Uncle Elephant got the ideas for his story.

## During Reading

Pause after reading the part of the story in which the lion roars, "A king and a prince! Just what I want for dinner!" Ask children to guess what they think could happen next in Uncle Elephant's story.

## After Reading

Discuss the similarities between Uncle Elephant and the little elephant and the king and prince of Uncle Elephant's story. Explain that many real-life authors do this. They base their story characters on themselves and their story plots on their own experiences but then use their imagination to add to and embellish their stories.

## Author's Craft

### Story Within a Story

#### (Exploring Story Structure)

This chapter is really a story within a story. With children, make a graphic organizer to show how this works. Draw a frame on chart paper. Ask, "Why does Uncle Elephant tell this story?" (*to forget his creaks*) Write the answer at the top of the frame. Then ask, "What happens at the very end of this chapter?" Write the answer at the bottom of the frame. Now elicit a brief summary of the story Uncle Elephant tells. Write this inside the frame. Point out to children that they have made a picture of how this story within a story works.

Then repeat the process, but this time, have children write their own story within a story. Have them draw a similar frame on a sheet of blank paper. First, they should think of characters they want to write about. Then at the top they should write down an idea of what might prompt one character to start telling a story. Inside the frame they will jot down a summary of a story. Then, at the bottom of the frame, have them write an ending that mirrors the beginning. Encourage children to draft full versions of their story within a story.

## Extending the Story

### Lift-the-Flap Story Crowns

(Identifying Story Elements)

Use the structure of Uncle Elephant's story as the basis for helping students identify key story elements.

1. Give each student a sheet of 11- by 17-inch paper. Model how to fold the paper in half lengthwise and then fold it into fourths.

2. Cut a triangle shape in the open edges, as shown.

3. Unfold the paper. Then make three cuts along the folds in the top half to create four flaps.

4. Have students label the top flaps "character," "setting," "problem," and "solution."

5. Underneath each flap, have children write or draw pictures to tell about each. Point out that there may be more than one problem in a story.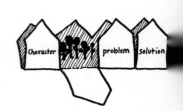

Uncle Elephant wants to forget his creaks.

Story he tells:
The king and the prince get lost.
A lion jumps out at them.
They scare him away.
The prince climbs on the king's shoulders.
They see the castle.
They go back home.

Uncle Elephant forgets his creaks.

# CHAPTER 7: "Uncle Elephant Wears His Clothes"

### Before Reading

Ask children to share ideas about things they might do or have done that have cheered them up when they felt sad. Tell them that in this story Uncle Elephant is going to try to cheer up the little elephant.

### During Reading

Ask children to explain how what Uncle Elephant is doing will help the little elephant forget his troubles.

### After Reading

✳ Ask, "Why was the little elephant so sad? What did Uncle Elephant do to make him feel better?"

✳ To add extra fun to a rereading of this chapter, bring in an assortment of clothing. When they reach the part of the story in which Uncle Elephant dons all his clothing, invite children to put on the clothes!

### Extending the Story

## Family Word Wall

(Building Vocabulary)

*Uncle Elephant* includes names for several people in families. Ask children to look through the book for examples (*mother, father, uncle, nephew*). What other family words do children know? (for example, *daughter, son*) Also ask children if they have special names for some family members, such as *nanny* or *gram* for grandmother or *pop* or *daddy* for father. Start a word wall of names for family members, and invite children to add to it and use these words in their writing.

## Character Clothing (Making Inferences)

Encourage children to think about the character of Uncle Elephant. Give each child a copy of page 66. (Enlarge the page, if desired.)

Divide the class into small groups and ask children to think about Uncle Elephant's character traits. Ask, "What words could you use to describe Uncle Elephant?" (for example, *caring, old, good storyteller, singer*) Ask children to find examples from the book that support their descriptions.

Then have them cut out the jacket from the activity page and fill in the blank lines, writing examples of character traits on the lines to the left and supporting examples from the book on the lines to the right. Children might describe incidents that show Uncle Elephant demonstrating the trait or use actual quotations from Uncle Elephant.

Afterward, string a clothesline across a corner of your classroom (or bulletin board) and use clothespins to clip up children's patterns. Bring the class together and invite children to share their responses.

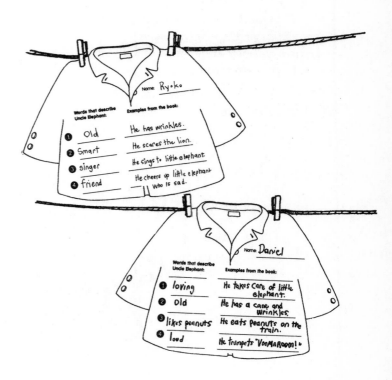

# CHAPTER 8: "Uncle Elephant Writes a Song"

## Before Reading

What songs do children know? Invite volunteers to sing a few lines to the class. Then tell children that this chapter is about a song that Uncle Elephant writes for the little elephant.

## During Reading

As children read this chapter, have them think about the idea that Uncle Elephant's song is a duet. Explain that a duet is a song sung or instruments played by two people. Encourage children to notice where the word *duet* appears in the chapter. Discuss why Uncle Elephant says there is no better music than a duet between an uncle and a nephew. Why is it fun to play music or sing together?

## After Reading

✻ Say to children, "At the beginning of this chapter, Uncle Elephant asks the little elephant to sing a song for him. Why do you think he does this? What is the result?"

✻ In the words to his song, Uncle Elephant describes different things he will be doing whenever he sings it. Which one seems the most fun to children, and why?

## Extending the Story

### Amazing Adjective Jar
(Word Study)

Have children locate the adjective *peanutty* in the chapter. Point out that the author creatively made this adjective or describing word from another word *peanut*. Have children create their own unusual adjectives and put them in a jar labeled "Amazing Adjectives." Then have them choose a word from the jar and write sentences using the adjective.

## Author's Craft

### Chime in With a Rhyme
(Using Colorful Language)

In the lyrics to Uncle Elephant's song, the author uses physical characteristics of Uncle Elephant as the basis for colorful rhyming phrases. These phrases translate into strong visual pictures:

● "With my trunk in a loop, I will sing while I swoop,"

● "Upside down on my head, with my ears as a sled,"

Challenge children to write and illustrate other colorful rhyming phrases to add to his song. For example:

● I can row with toes while the sea flows.

● With bells on my feet, my song will sound sweet!

● With my trunk I will toot, just like a flute!

With my trunk I will toot, just like a flute!

# CHAPTER 9: "Uncle Elephant Closes the Door"

## Before Reading

Have children talk about how this story might end. Ask, "Will the little elephant stay with Uncle Elephant? What might happen that would make the little elephant leave his uncle? Do you think the story will have a happy ending?"

## During Reading

❋ Ask children whether anyone knows what a telegram is. Explain that long ago, before telephones or e-mail made it easy for people to communicate with each other, telegrams were a way for people to send short written messages that arrived more quickly than regular mail.

❋ Pause after the little elephant tells his uncle he thinks he is counting the telephone poles. Ask, "What do you think Uncle Elephant is counting?"

## After Reading

Ask children what they think about the ending. How would they feel if they were the little elephant? Then have them go back and read the titles of the first and last chapters. Ask, "Why do you think the author chose these chapter titles to begin and end the book?"

## Extending the Story

### Story Caboose (Summarizing)

Encourage children to compare what happens at the end of the story with the predictions they made. Talk about the feelings that Uncle Elephant and the little elephant have at the end of their time together. You might use this as an opportunity to have children think about how feelings can often be mixed and complex. Ask, "Is this mainly a happy ending? What about the ending is also sad?" Add the story ending in the caboose on the Story Train (see pages 55 and 64).

## All Aboard! (Building Fluency, Art)

Help children build reading fluency by pairing up to practice reading this chapter aloud. To add to the experience, let children make stick puppets of Uncle Elephant and the little elephant and put them aboard their very own trains!

Collect empty cookie or cake boxes that have cellophane windows. Provide children with art materials such as colored tape, construction paper, fabric scraps, glue, crayons, and markers. Then help them follow these steps:

**1.** Tape a box closed. Use strips of colored tape or construction paper to divide the cellophane window into separate train windows.

**2.** Add decorative details such as curtains, wheels, and doors.

**3.** Have children make their stick puppets (using index cards, tape, and craft sticks) after making their trains to gauge how big the puppets can be.

**4.** To put their puppets aboard the train, turn the box on its side as shown. Help children cut slits in what is now the bottom of the box, through which they can slide their puppets.

**5.** Invite one child to read the story while the other child manipulates the puppets and the train. Then have them switch places.

# Story Train

Fill in the story train with the parts of the story.

Title

*Teaching With Favorite Arnold Lobel Books*    Scholastic Teaching Resou

I wish

Magic Lamp
Wish Book

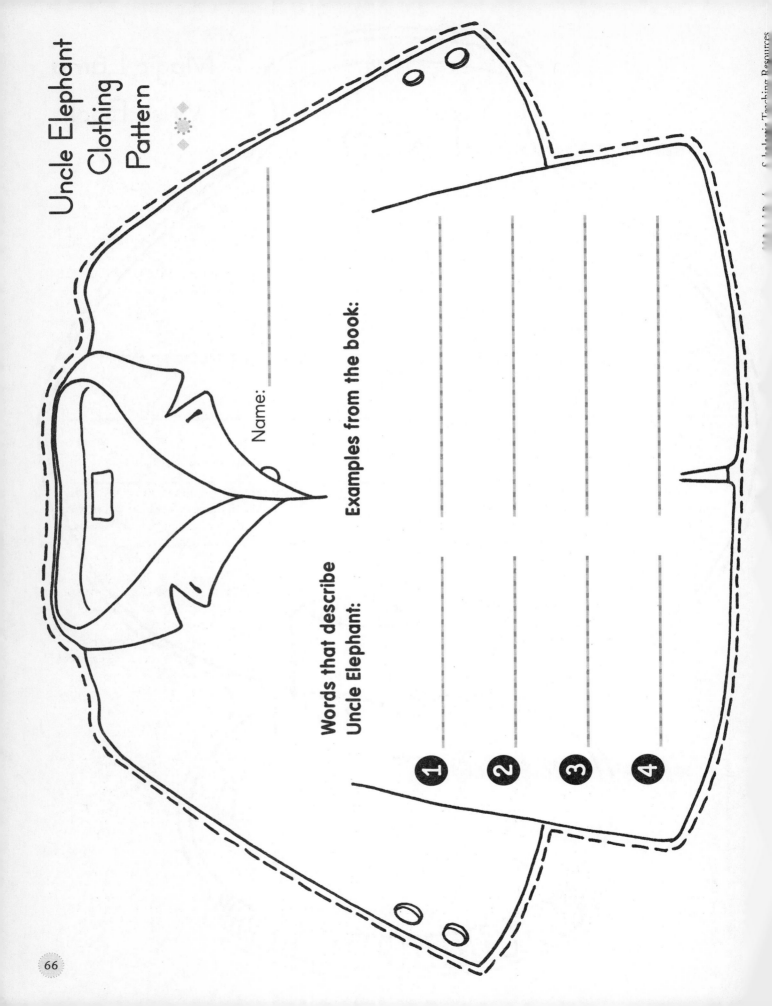

Uncle Elephant
Clothing
Pattern

Name: _____

**Examples from the book:**

**Words that describe
Uncle Elephant:**

1

2

3

4

# Tying It All Together

## First-Person Narratives (Writing)

Invite children to write first-person narratives about an experience with an older person. First review the elements of a first-person narrative. Explain that you are the one telling the story, and it is about something real that has happened to you. You write it using the pronouns *I, me,* and *my.* To help children frame an experience to write about, offer these prompts:

◎ "Think of something that you did with someone who is older than you, such as visiting an older relative, or going shopping with an older friend."

◎ "What was the most fun or interesting part of what you did?"

◎ "What did you learn from the older person?"

## Memory Trunk (Identifying Details, Art)

When the time comes for the little elephant to return home, he has a wealth of rich memories of his times with Uncle Elephant—enough to fill a trunk! Invite children to pack a memory trunk for the little elephant and fill it with reminders of the times he shared with Uncle Elephant.

First, go through the book with children and ask them to name things that the little elephant and Uncle Elephant did together. What kinds of mementos or pictures might the little elephant want to pack in his trunk to remember these times? (*peanuts, a lamp, flowers, a flower crown, a copy of Uncle Elephant's song, and so on*)

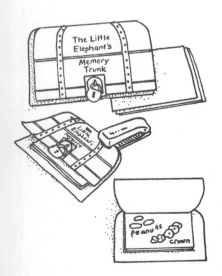

Then give each child a copy of the trunk pattern on page 68 to color, cut out, and fold in half along the solid line. Give them several quarter sheets of paper to staple inside the trunk. Tell them to draw or paste and label things on the pages that the little elephant might put in his trunk. Invite children to share their memory trunks and talk about why they chose each item.

## Mood Meter (Making Inferences)

From chapter to chapter, the little elephant's emotions undergo many changes. Help children monitor these changes with this graphic organizer. Give each child a copy of page 69, scissors, and a brass fastener. Have children cut out the patterns and assemble as shown.

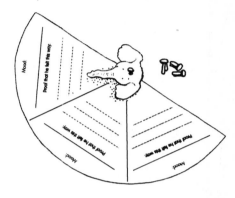

Then talk with children about the feelings the little elephant experienced at different parts in the book (for example, *sad, happy, excited, afraid, curious*).

Have children choose three different emotions and write them on the meter. Encourage them to find specific places in the book that explain or show why he felt each way and write about them. (You may wish to make multiple copies of the reproducible and have children do this activity for separate chapters.)

Invite children to share what they wrote, moving the pointer to each mood as they do so.

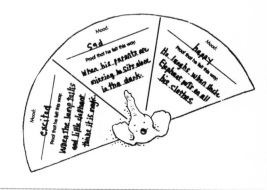

Mood Meter activity adapted from *Quick & Creative Reading Response Activities* by Jane Fowler and Stephanie Newlon (Scholastic, 2003).

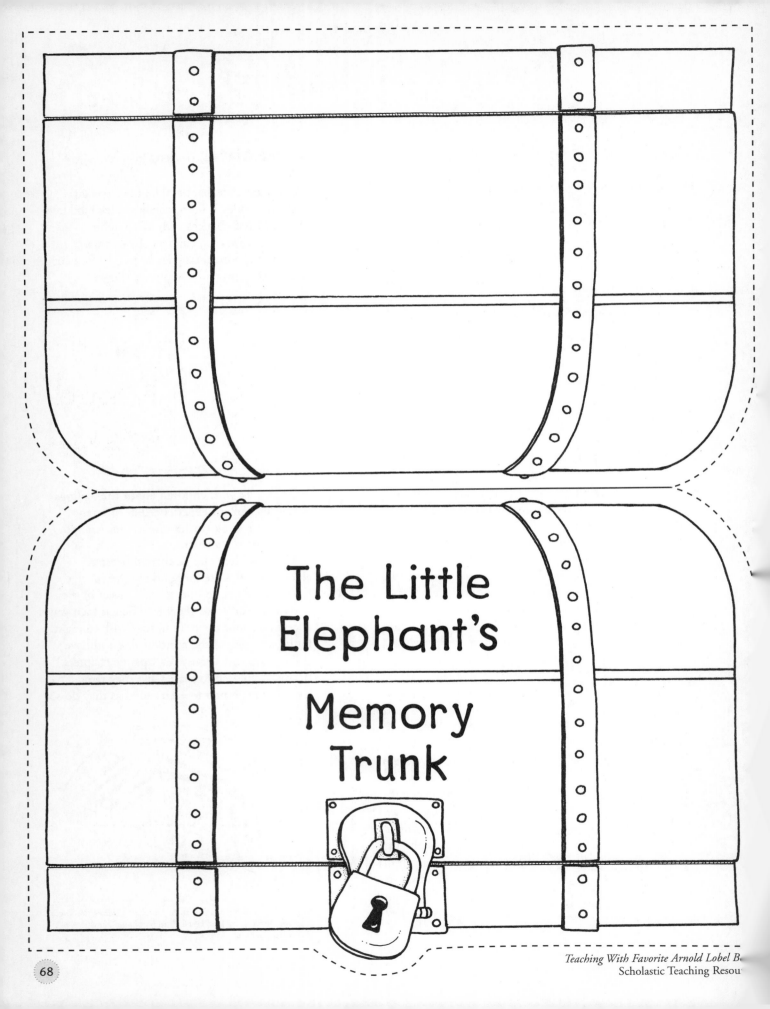

The Little Elephant's

Memory Trunk

*Teaching With Favorite Arnold Lobel B*
Scholastic Teaching Resou

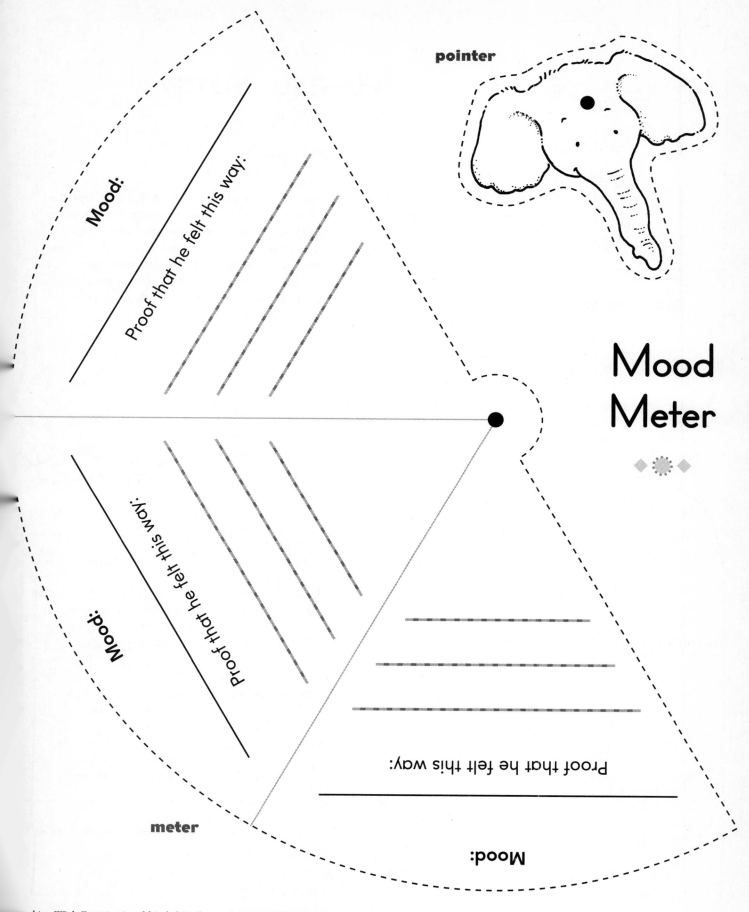

**pointer**

# Mood Meter

◆ ✳ ◆

Mood:

Proof that he felt this way:

Mood:

Proof that he felt this way:

**meter**

Proof that he felt this way:

Mood:

# Mouse Soup

◆ ❋ ◆

(HARPERCOLLINS, 1977)

**M**ouse Soup is a clever takeoff on *1001 Arabian Nights*. In this case, instead of Scheherazade telling stories to the king to save her life, the mouse tells the weasel stories to distract him from making mouse soup. With this as the jumping-off point, Arnold Lobel concocts four of his most delightful stories, each with a charming twist. At the end of the book, the mouse tricks the weasel into leaving in search of story elements for his soup, giving the mouse a chance to escape. *Mouse Soup* provides children with a captivating entre into the nourishing world of stories and storytelling.

## Threading Through the Book

After reading the introduction, discuss the solution that the mouse finds. Ask, "Were you surprised by the mouse's idea? How do you think it will help the mouse to tell the weasel that the soup must be mixed with stories?" Help children to see that the mouse has predicted exactly how the weasel will respond. Then ask, "How do you think it will help the mouse to tell stories to the weasel?"

## Mouse Tricks Chart

(Identifying Problems and Solutions)

The way that the mice use their wits to solve a problem in each story makes *Mouse Soup* a perfect tool for helping children improve their comprehension of problem and solution in stories. The problem may not always be what it seems on the surface. In "The Thorn Bush," for example, at first it looks as if having a thorn bush grow in a chair is an awful state of affairs, but then we learn that the old lady mouse is actually upset because her thorn bush isn't healthy.

Identifying the problems and solutions will help children better

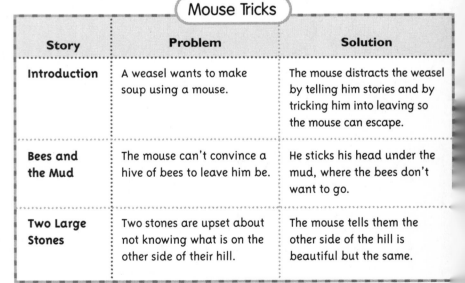

### Mouse Tricks

| Story | Problem | Solution |
|---|---|---|
| **Introduction** | A weasel wants to make soup using a mouse. | The mouse distracts the weasel by telling him stories and by tricking him into leaving so the mouse can escape. |
| **Bees and the Mud** | The mouse can't convince a hive of bees to leave him be. | He sticks his head under the mud, where the bees don't want to go. |
| **Two Large Stones** | Two stones are upset about not knowing what is on the other side of their hill. | The mouse tells them the other side of the hill is beautiful but the same. |

understand how they are connected. Keep an ongoing Mouse Tricks chart such as the one above, and have children fill in the chart after reading each story. (Fill in the solution to the problem established in the introduction when you finish the book.) To provide a deeper understanding, use the chart to generate discussion about each problem and solution.

Following are some questions and discussion points for the individual stories:

**"Bees and the Mud"**

✳ While reading, pause and ask, "Why do you think the mouse says, 'Here is my front door,' as he steps into the muddy swamp? Is this really his front door? Why might he say this to the bees?"

✳ "When do the bees notice there is something wrong? What do they do?"

✳ "How is ducking under the mud a good way for the mouse to get rid of the bees without being stung?"

**"Two Large Stones"**

✳ Discuss the different perspectives of the bird and the mouse regarding the other side of the hill. What does each animal see? Why are their views so different?

✳ Have children study the two illustrations of the rocks in which they feel alternately happy and sad. Ask, "How does one picture tell you that the rocks are sad? How does the other show that they are happy?"

✳ Talk about the expression, "The grass always looks greener on the other side of the hill." In this case, when the stones learn that their side of the hill looks just the same as the other side, they realize that their side is just as beautiful.

**"The Crickets"**

✳ Discuss what the cricket hears and does not hear of what the mouse is saying. How does hearing only this last part lead to the cricket's misunderstanding the mouse?

✳ Talk about how the mouse finally gets the cricket to be quiet. Point out that asking directly and clearly for something often has a good result.

**"The Thorn Bush"**

✳ How is this story similar to the last story children read? (*In "The Crickets," a character misunderstood what was said. In this story, a policeman misunderstands what he sees.*)

✳ What did the policeman think the problem was? What did it really turn out to be?

✳ "What might make the thorn bush better?"

## Story Starter Soup (Writing)

The soup in *Mouse Soup* is a fanciful one. Talk with children about what goes into a tasty soup (a variety of ingredients and spices). Ask, "How is real soup like a story soup? How is it different?"

Then set the stage for using the stories in this book as a springboard for writing by putting a big pot in your writing center. Provide a ladle or big spoon and a supply of adding machine paper strips (or use lasagna noodles and markers!).

Then ask children, "What other stories might the mouse have told the weasel?" Invite them to visit the center, write story ideas on the strips or noodles, and toss them in the soup pot. Once you have a good supply, let children take turns scooping out a story idea and using it as the basis for writing a new mouse story.

### Author's Craft

# Buzz Words
### (Using Onomatopoeia)

Remind children that in "Bees and the Mud," the bees *buzz*. In "The Crickets," the crickets *chirp*. Point out that these words sound like their meanings. With children, brainstorm a list of other animal sound words that sound like what they mean, such as *meow, click,* and *growl*.

Then start a word wall of onomatopoeic words. Let children take turns reading the words, giving them extra emphasis. Challenge children to be on the lookout when they read for other sound words to add to the list. (Examples in other Lobel stories include *thud* and *plop* from "Down the Hill" in *Frog and Toad All Year* and *voomarooom* from "Uncle Elephant Trumpets the Dawn" in *Uncle Elephant*.)

## Be Up on Your Bees!

(Science, Language Arts)

After reading "Bees and the Mud," ask children what they would like to find out about bees. On large index cards, have them write questions, such as:

✳ **What is a bee's nest called?**

✳ **How do bees make honey?**

✳ **Why do bees like flowers?**

✳ **Why do bee stings hurt? What should you do if you get stung by a bee?**

Help children look for the answers to their questions in various sources, such as science magazines, books, and the Internet. (Always supervise children's use of the Internet.) Tell children to write the answers to the questions on the backs of the cards. Then create a bulletin board display.

◎ Draw and cut out a large beehive shape from construction paper. On it write "Be Up on Your Bees!" Attach the hive to the wall at student height.

◎ Invite children to make models of bees, using yellow and black pipe cleaners. Have them leave a half pipe cleaner length on each bee.

◎ Punch a hole in the corner of each card and secure a pipe cleaner bee to each. Wrap the other end of the pipe cleaner around a pushpin. Then attach the bee cards to the hive.

Encourage children to read classmates' questions and then flip over the cards for the answers.

## Story Board Stones

(Retelling and Sequencing)

In "Two Large Stones," the two stones come full circle. At the beginning of the story, they are content with their side of the hill. In the middle they feel sad that they will never see what is on the other side. Finally, they come to appreciate the beauty of their side again.

Help children identify and sequence the key events in this story by completing the graphic organizer on page 73. Encourage them to use transition words such as *first, second, then, next,* and *finally* or *last.* If children have difficulty recalling the order, suggest that they start with the beginning and the end of the story and then go back to identify the important events that happened in the middle. Then have children complete the graphic organizer.

### Author's Craft

## A Bouquet of Words

(Adding Descriptive Details)

Have children reread the part of the story in "The Thorn Bush" in which the thorn bush starts to grow: "Green leaves came out of the branches. Little buds came out near the leaves. The buds opened up. They became large roses." Explain that *green* is a describing word, or adjective, and that it helps tell more about the naming word, or noun, *leaves.* Can children find other examples of describing words in this passage? (*Little* describes *buds. Large* describes *roses.*) Ask children what the describing words do. (*tell more about something or tell one thing from another*) At the top of a sheet of chart paper, write the words *leaves* and *buds.* Ask children to list adjectives that tell more about these words.

| Leaves | Buds |
|--------|------|
| pointy | big |
| maple | pink |
| fall | tiny |

Then give each child a copy of page 74. Have children write the word *rose* in the center flower. Let children work together to come up with words that might be used to describe a rose (*beautiful, red, sweet-smelling,* and so on), and write these inside each of the remaining roses.

# Story Board
## Stones

Name _____

**Title of Story** _____

Draw or write the main events of this story.
Put them in the correct order.

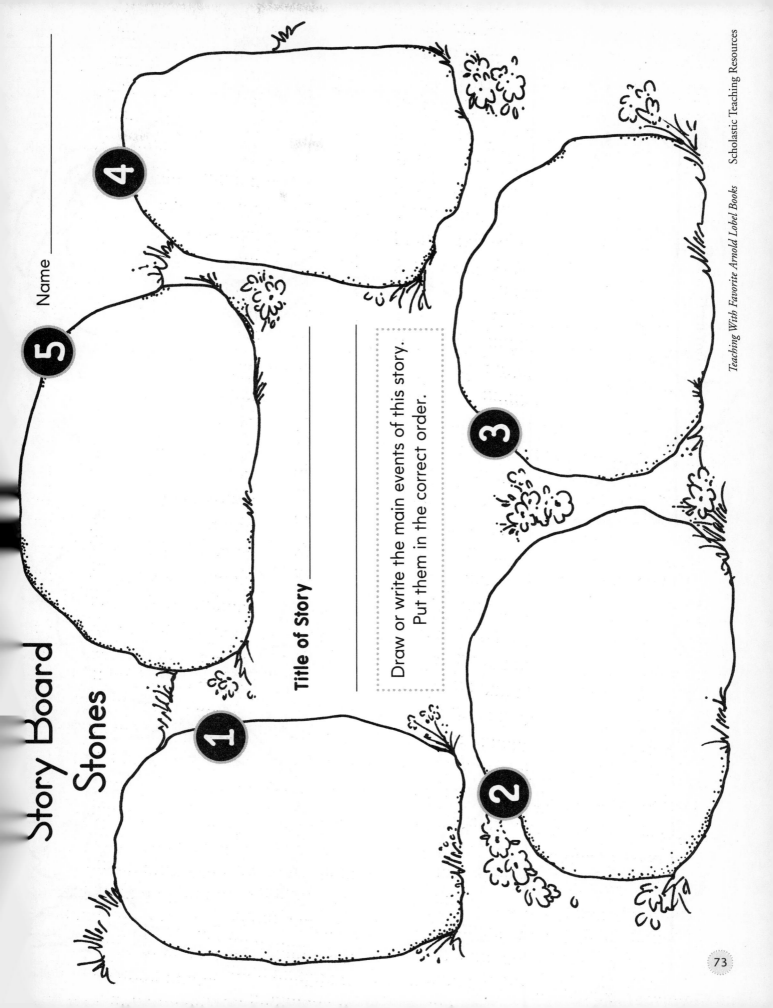

*Teaching With Favorite Arnold Lobel Books*    Scholastic Teaching Resources

# A Bouquet of Words

*Teaching With Favorite Arnold Lobel Books*    Scholastic Teaching Re

# Tying It All Together

## Follow That Book!
(Exploring Theme)

In the introduction to *Mouse Soup*, Arnold Lobel uses imaginative illustrations to bring alive his theme of the importance of reading stories. Children may not have taken note that on each page that the mouse appears, he is holding tightly to his precious book. Use the following hints to help children track the illustrations.

✳ "On the opening page, see how the mouse is reading the book under the tree? Let's skim through *Mouse Soup* and keep track of what happens to that book."

✳ "Now the weasel has caught the mouse (page 9). What's happened to the book? Why do you think the mouse didn't just let go of it?"

✳ "Let's study the page where the weasel is starting up the soup (page 10). What is the mouse doing with his book now?"

✳ "Let's look at the little picture of the mouse in the soup at the beginning of 'Bees and the Mud.' Can we find the book? Now let's check the beginning of each of the other stories."

✳ "Does the mouse still have the book with him when he sends the weasel out to hunt for stories? What happens to the book at the end?"

Elicit from children that the mouse has worked very hard to keep the book with him at all times and that he is happy to be back home and be able to finish reading it at the end.

## Finish the Mouse Tricks Chart
(Identifying Problems and Solutions)

After reading the ending of *Mouse Soup*, engage children in a discussion of what happens. Ask, "How did the mouse use the stories to get the weasel to go away? What happens to the weasel? How is this a clever solution to the problem?" Have children complete the Mouse Tricks chart (page 70). Then talk about the chart as a whole. Discuss how the problems and solutions are similar and how they are different.

## Story Weaving (Oral Language, Listening)

Have children sit in a circle. Provide a ball of yarn or string. Begin a story by saying a sentence aloud. Use a classic folktale opening, such as "Once upon a time there was a fisherman who lived by the ocean" or "Once there was an owl that lived in the forest." Then toss the ball to a child. Have that child add a sentence to the story. The child who adds the sentence tosses the ball to another child. Each child holds the end of yarn or string so that a web is made. As you weave your story, you may wish to tape-record or write it on a sheet of chart paper. Discuss with children how this process is similar to the way stories get handed down orally.

Activity Page

## Write a Story
(Exploring Problems and Solutions)

Use page 76 to give children practice writing a short story that has a problem and a solution. First, read the story starter with children. Ask them to use their imagination to think about what might happen next. Then have them complete the page. Afterward, invite children to share their stories with classmates.

Name _____ Date _____

# Write a Story

Finish this story in your own words. Add a picture, too.

One day the mouse woke up and it was raining outside. But he just had to go to the store for some cheese. He looked all over the house for an umbrella. But he couldn't find one. He looked for a raincoat. But he couldn't find one. He looked for a rain hat. But he couldn't find one.

So he _____

_____

_____

_____

**What is the problem in the story you wrote?**

_____

_____

**What is the solution?**

_____

_____

# Fables

◆ ❋ ◆

(HARPERCOLLINS, 1980)

When Arnold Lobel turns his hand to writing fables, the result is witty, original, and imaginative—everything that makes his work unique. Like most fables, these feature animal characters that have human characteristics. We encounter a camel that yearns to become a ballet dancer, a father-and-son conflict between elephants, a kangaroo who is bad in school, and more. At the end of each is the moral that is the fable's signature. But the morals are not always so obvious in Arnold Lobel's fables; instead they provide an unexpected twist that adds depth and humor to these wonderful stories.

## Book Talk

To discuss the fables, you may wish to divide the class into small groups or pairs for literature circles. Have each circle talk about one or more of the fables. Encourage them to discuss and take notes about some of the following:

❋ "How do the characters in this fable seem like real animals? How do they seem like people? Does anything happen that could never happen in real life? What happens that does seem like real life?"

❋ "Were you surprised by the moral or lesson learned at the end of the fable? Why or why not?"

❋ "Tell about anything that has happened to you or that you have read about that is like what happens in this fable."

Afterward, bring the class together to share their responses. You might also want to have children compare Lobel's fables with those of Aesop or other classic fables.

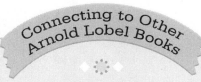

### Connecting to Other Arnold Lobel Books

◆ ❋ ◆

The characters in *Fables* will strongly remind children of themselves and their own experiences. It is useful to compare these fables to other works by Arnold Lobel, especially the Frog and Toad series. Point out how the life lessons found in the Frog and Toad books are very similar to the morals of these fables.

## Extending the Stories

### Write a Fable (Writing)

Have children choose one of the fables to use as a model in writing their own fable.

**1.** Suggest that children choose one or two favorite animals to "star" in their fable. Have them list characteristics that these animals have in real life. Then encourage them to brainstorm other ways that these animals could act—for instance, a peacock could be vain or a walrus could be silly.

**2.** Invite children to choose a favorite fable from Arnold Lobel's collection. Ask them to analyze this fable, figuring out how the moral sums up what happens and looking at how the animals behave.

**3.** Tell children to draft a story that illustrates the same moral, using animal characters from their list.

**4.** Have children work in small groups or pairs to look at and critique each other's work, asking questions, such as

❋ "Does the moral of this fable make sense with what happens in the story? Did you write about animal characters that combined real life and fantasy?"

❋ Suggest that children revise their drafts based on the discussion.

# Ming Lo Moves the Mountain

## (GREENWILLOW BOOKS, 1982)

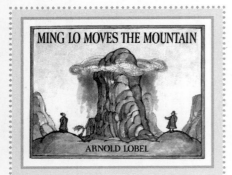

**M**ing Lo isn't very happy living next to a mountain. Rocks are always falling on his roof, the sun never reaches his garden, and constant rainfall makes home life damp and miserable. So Ming Lo and his wife visit the wise man to find a way to move the mountain. And surprisingly they do!

*Ming Lo Moves the Mountain* is an original story with all the elements of a classic folktale. You can use this book to explore a simple problem and solution story structure. The story also contains many elements that children will recognize as classic Lobel. The silliness of the premise (to want to move a mountain) combined with the truth and simplicity of the resolution (the trick is to move oneself) is a familiar feature in Lobel's stories.

### Book Talk

As you read the book, stop to ask:

✳ "Why does Ming Lo want to move the mountain? What would be an easier way for Ming Lo to get away from the mountain?"

✳ "What kind of person would you say Ming Lo is? What do you think about his decision to move the mountain?"

After reading, discuss the story:

✳ "Was the wise man's solution to Ming Lo's problem wise? Why or why not?"

✳ "What did Ming Lo learn in the end?"

### Extending the Story

## Ask the Wise People
(Drama, Problem Solving)

Invite the class to act out the story and to use it in building new story scenes. However, instead of one wise person, let your class version feature many wise people. These wise people can offer new and even sillier solutions to Ming Lo's problem. Assign the roles of narrator, Ming Lo and his wife, and wise people. Ming Lo and his wife can visit a new wise person after every failed attempt to move the mountain. The last wise person can be the one who offers the "true" solution.

## Scroll Paintings/Calligraphy
(Social Studies, Art)

*Ming Lo Moves the Mountain* is filled with beautiful illustrations of an ancient Chinese landscape based on traditional Chinese paintings. Invite children to make their own Chinese scroll painting of Ming Lo's world, which they can label with Chinese calligraphic symbols. If possible, show children samples of Chinese landscape painting (on the Internet go to the Web site of the Metropolitan Museum of Art: www.metmuseum.org/toah/hd/clpg/hd/clpg.htm) and calligraphy (go to the Chinese Symbols Clip-Art Collection: www.formosa-translation.com/chinese/).

Give children long thin pieces of paper. Set out watercolor paints, crayons, and other art materials. Have children look through *Ming Lo Moves the Mountain* to pick out a few things to include in their pictures (for example, a mountain, a tree, a bird, and a Chinese-style house).

After they have painted and drawn their objects, invite children to label them using Chinese calligraphic symbols. Then roll their scroll paintings up and tie them with ribbon.

### Connecting to Other Arnold Lobel Books

**A** *Treeful of Pigs* (Greenwillow Books, 1979) is a good companion to *Ming Lo Moves the Mountain*. It has elements of a folktale, particularly a fable, but combines this with some elements of fantasy stories, too. Like fables, it teaches a lesson about life.

# Mouse Tales

◆❋◆

( H A R P E R C O L L I N S ,  1 9 7 2 )

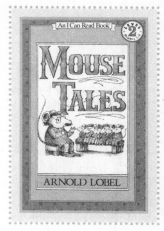

**S**even mice lying awake in bed ask their father to tell them a story to help them sleep. This opening provides the frame for the seven charming mouse tales that follow. Each one is different, but all involve mice as the main characters. At the end of the book, the mice children have fallen fast asleep by listening to these wonderful tales.

While each of the mouse tales seems simple on the surface, by looking closely at them, children can unravel the delightful twist in each one. They are a good companion to *Mouse Soup*.

## Book Talk

Have children practice summarizing stories by answering these questions for each of the tales:

❋ "What are the characters in this tale?"

❋ "What is the most important thing that happens in this tale?"

❋ "What surprised you most when you read this tale?"

## Extending the Stories

## Pick a Tale (Exploring Story Elements)

Help children write and illustrate their own mouse tales. Create two boxes and label one "Characters" and the other "Settings."

◉ On note cards, write specific descriptions for mouse characters, such as "cowboy mouse," and "city mouse." Make sure there is at least one description for each child. Place these in the Characters box.

◉ On additional note cards, write specific settings that could be a spark for a story, such as "snowstorm," "walk in the woods," and "schoolroom." Place these in the Settings box.

◉ Have each child choose one card from each of the boxes. It may help to have children work in pairs or small groups to brainstorm ideas. Then have them write a draft of a short tale.

◉ Encourage children to look at the illustration style in "The Mouse and the Winds" and "The Journey" and notice how the illustrations are intermingled with the text. Have them rewrite a final draft and illustrate their tales.

## String a Story (Retelling and Sequencing)

Help children practice retelling skills with this activity.

**1.** Divide the class into seven groups. Assign one tale to each group.

**2.** Punch two holes at the top of large unlined index cards.

**3.** Tell children that they are to retell their story by illustrating on the cards the beginning, middle (or key events), and end. Encourage children to use transition words such as *first, then, next,* and *finally* or *last.*

**4.** Have each group string the cards, in order, through a length of yarn.

**5.** Invite each group to retell their story to the class.

# Celebrating Arnold Lobel

**E**nding an author study on Arnold Lobel is like saying good-bye to a lot of very good friends. Here are a few activities to help you remember and say good-bye to Frog and Toad, Owl, Uncle Elephant, Grasshopper, and other new friends.

## Cookie and Character Party

Invite children to reflect on their favorite characters while engaging in an activity that evokes the homeyness of Arnold Lobel's stories: having a cookie and character party!

Ask children to write their favorite Lobel character on a slip of paper. On the other side, have them write a reason that they liked the character or a favorite thing the character did. Have children drop their responses in a paper bag.

Then pass a plate of cookies around in one direction while passing the bag in the other direction. As the plate and bag come around, children can take a cookie and a classmate's response to read and share with the class.

## Character Pair-Ups

What if Toad spent a day at Owl's house? Or the little elephant traveled with Grasshopper? How would the personality of each character contribute to the kinds of problems and adventures that might result from such character pair-ups? Have children team up with a classmate and each choose a character from a different book. Invite them to prepare presentations for the class. Before they begin, children might find it useful to prepare a Venn Diagram that compares and contrasts the two characters. Suggested formats follow:

◎ **Spin a Story:** Invite children to write and illustrate a short story featuring their characters.

◎ **Perform a Play:** Have children each take the part of a character and act out a short scene.

◎ **Create a Comic Strip:** Invite children to write and illustrate a comic strip with dialogue balloons starring the two characters.

◎ **Put on a Puppet Show:** Let children make craft stick puppets to represent each character and perform a skit.

◎ **Pen a Poem:** Challenge children to write a poem about the two characters.

## Arnold Lobel's Favorite Things

Another fitting and fun way to celebrate the end of your author study is to hold an Arnold Lobel's Favorite Things Guessing Game. Many of Lobel's best stories center on an everyday object. Even the story titles—"The Button," "The Hat," "Two Large Stones"—suggest the importance of such objects in the worlds of his stories. Invite children to recall their favorite stories by focusing on such key objects.

**1.** Ask children to choose a significant object from one of the stories. (Or, to ensure that the activity includes a variety of different objects, write the names of objects on slips of paper yourself and give one to each child.)

**2.** Have children either find or make a simple drawing of their object.

**3.** Tell them to create a written clue for their object that will help others guess the story it is from. For example, "Owl cried into me." (teapot from "Tear-Water Tea" in *Owl at Home*); "Uncle Elephant tried to count us." (telephone poles from "Uncle Elephant Counts the Poles" in *Uncle Elephant*)

**4.** Collect children's drawings and objects. Gather children in a circle and place their drawings and objects in the center. Let children take turns reading aloud their clues while classmates try to pick out the object or picture.